National Accounts and Economic Value

National Accounts and Economic Value

A Study in Concepts

Utz-Peter Reich

palgrave

First published 2001 by
PALGRAVE
Houndmills, Basingstoke, Hampshire RG21 6XS and
175 Fifth Avenue, New York, N. Y. 10010
Companies and representatives throughout the world

PALGRAVE is the new global academic imprint of
St. Martin's Press LLC Scholarly and Reference Division and
Palgrave Publishers Ltd (formerly Macmillan Press Ltd).

ISBN 0–333–73391–6

This book is printed on paper suitable for recycling and made from fully managed and sustained forest sources.

A catalogue record for this book is available from the British Library.

Library of Congress Cataloging-in-Publication Data
Reich, Utz-Peter.
    National accounts and economic value : a study in concepts /
Utz-Peter Reich.
        p. cm.
    Includes bibliographical references and index.
    ISBN 0–333–73391–6
    1. Value. 2. Microeconomics. 3. Economics. I. Title.

    HB201 .R395 2001
    339.3—dc21
                                                            2001021637

10   9   8   7   6   5   4   3   2   1
10 09 08 07 06 05 04 03 02 01

Printed and bound in Great Britain by
Antony Rowe Ltd, Chippenham, Wiltshire

*To **András Bródy**, my teacher in value theory,*
*and **Richard Ruggles**, my teacher in national accounts*

Contents

1
Introduction: Why Write About Value in the Context of National Accounts?

The purpose of combining national accounts and the theory of economic value is explained in this chapter. The main argument is that the concepts of a theory should comply with the standards of their measurement, which in economics are those of accounting.

A book is written to promote knowledge and truth, but it will open minds only if it is entertaining. Thus, dear reader, my wish is to entertain you.

Value theory tells us what is good and how good it is, what we appreciate and why, and that all these value judgements are actually measured in our economy and how this is done. What is wealth, and what is well-being? Why are we willing to spend money on something, and what is really spent if money is spent? Economic and moral questions seem to be inseparable in practice.

There are some conflicts between statistics and economics, conflicts such as the one exemplified by a famous hunting conundrum:

> If it usually costs twice the labour to kill a beaver which it does to kill a deer, one beaver should naturally exchange for or be worth two deer? It is natural that what is usually the produce of two days, or two hours, labour should be worth double of what is usually the product of one day's or one hour's labour.

This law of value is from Adam Smith (1776), the founding father of our economics science.[1] As economists, however, we have been trained to reject this thesis, or more precisely to accept it only on the condition that the average cost equals the marginal cost of hunting these animals and this in turn equals the marginal utility of eating them. This value theory is firmly established in first-year economics. However if you want to put the theory to statistical test with the help of the national accounts, you may find the price of the beaver and the price of the deer in the accounts, but there will be no reference to marginal cost or marginal utility to explain them. You may even find that the prices are estimated on the basis of hours worked without any knowledge of marginal cost or utility conditions. More generally, it seems that the national accounts do not submit to the marginal theory of value, and it may be entertaining to investigate this.

As scientists we have been trained to view measurement as a means of providing objectivity. A measured figure is true and provides knowledge, we are told, unlike value judgements, which are immeasurable. Thus to say that a beaver should cost twice as much as a deer is rejected as a scientific statement because it is a value judgement. But if in the process of establishing a national price for beaver the price observer, on her or his visit to the butcher, finds the beaver to be of much lower quality than before, and acts accordingly, is that not a value judgement? The interesting question here is: what has economic theory to offer in respect of the norms and objectivity that are involved in measuring an economic figure? National accountants have come to the point where they politely say 'Not much'.

Since the most satisfying way of entertaining an audience is through beauty, this book also makes an effort in that direction. The beauty of a theoretical construct is its simplicity. To be able to prove that a number of consumers with individual preferences and a number of producers of different goods and services can be joined in a common equilibrium of quoted prices and quantities produced and consumed is a beauty of intellectual insight that has stimulated the advancement of microeconomic theory in many directions. In a similar fashion, this book endeavours to reveal the beauty of the national accounts – , contained in their axiomatic reconstruction – and to advertise it to the general economist.

It must be said – and deplored – that the disciplines of economics and national accounting have parted. At the beginning of the national accounts project many great theorists put their minds to the national accounts, and helped to bring them to life but today the topic is almost forgotten in economic research and teaching. It is treated as purely technical and of no further theoretical interest. This is practical in many respects, but in the field of value theory the discrepancies are too strong to be left unattended.

It so happens that there is only one laboratory for the economist – the current economy – and there is only one tool for measuring the latter – the national accounts. So any economist who wants to use figures must use the national accounts. Whatever theory of value economists have in mind or want to prove when working with such figures, they are constrained to the meaning that national accountants have imposed on them when trying to make a representation of the economy that can be called true. Not to understand the operations through which the numbers have been established is like standing in a kitchen and seeing how much of a substance is in a jar, but not knowing what that substance is. Public discussions of a green national product or the government deficit have largely been nourished by such lack of understanding.

The 1993 SNA (the system of national accounts adopted by the five major international economic organisations), with over 700 pages, is an intractable piece of work and far too heavy to take to an economic conference. But at the same time it is the edifice within which every economic phenomenon is housed, and will continue to be housed in the future. It will hardly be fully read or understood by any one person, but it will provide the basis of study for many. And it has a silent message: it hints that the microeconomic theory of value is insufficient for guiding and interpreting the national accounts.

What is unsatisfactory about the microeconomic theory of value for national accounting? It cannot be lack of beauty, because the general equilibrium model is as beautiful as Euclidian geometry. The difference between the two is that the latter incorporates a prescription for measurement whereas the former does not. Rulers and compasses are handed to students of geometry from their first day. Microeconomics, however, does not even deal with cardinal numbers, much less provide the tools to establish them.

The disappointment of national accountants and statistical practitioners with the microeconomic theory of value derives from the failure of its concepts to operate at the macroeconomic level. Let us look at two cases in point. The microeconomic model is based on the concept of a fully homogeneous commodity. This means that wheat in Chicago is a different commodity from wheat in New York, and that wheat today is different from wheat tomorrow. Applying this idea to the national accounts makes measurement virtually impossible. The accounts are based on the assumption that these four microcommodities are actually a single commodity observed under different circumstances. Otherwise there can be no aggregation in space or over time. Another problematic concept is that of money. Money is not needed to define value in microeconomic theory, as value is defined only in terms of relative prices. Money works simply as a numéraire and can be replaced by any other commodity. There is no explanation of the absolute price of a commodity on the market. But absolute prices are what statisticians find at their commodity outlets, and what they must explain. They need a value theory of absolute prices.

Where, then, are we heading in this book? Let us point the way with an analogy. When in the eighteenth century the science of mechanics triumphed over religion the French mathematician Laplace proposed an ideal of mechanics. If one could determine the location, q, and momentum, p, of all particles of matter one would be able to predict the future of the world. The general equilibrium model is of the same ilk, with the quantity q, and price, p, of an almost infinite number of commodities determining the state of an economy. Physics subsequently turned to thermodynamics, where new variables such as pressure, volume and temperature were defined for the macro level of investigation but had no meaning for an individual particle. In a similar way practical economics has turned to the national accounts statistics to measure and define its macro variables, and it is not evident that micro variables have a place there. At any rate, it is appropriate that the theory of value should follow suit.

Fortunately we are not alone in this endeavour. We need not postulate a new theory, merely recover what others have crafted before us. The micro-economic theory of value followed on the heels of classical value theory, which has since lived in the shadows of the theoretical mainstream. The striking conceptual departure with which the marginalist theory of value buried its predecessor is captured by another famous quotation from Adam Smith:

> The word value, it is to be observed, has two different meanings, and sometimes expresses the utility of some particular object, and sometimes the power of purchasing other goods which the possession of that object conveys. The one may be called 'value in use'; the other 'value in exchange'. The things which have the greatest value in use have frequently little or no value in exchange; and, on the contrary, those which have the greatest value in exchange have frequently little or no value in use. Nothing is more useful than water but it will purchase scarce anything; scarce anything can be had in exchange for it. A diamond, on the contrary, has scarce any value in use but a very great quantity of other goods may frequently be had in exchange for it.[2]

Before we decide whether this paradox be explained by Gossen's laws, let us pose a question. In what units is the comparison made? Can we generalise the above to other commodities and ask, for example, whether flowers have greater purchasing power than flour, or bricks have less purchasing power than beds? Generally speaking, is it meaningful to compare prices between goods and describe them as lower or higher, given that each price refers to a different physical unit? This is the reason, incidentally, for which the micro-economic commodity space cannot really be called Euclidian. As each dimension is subject to a different unit of measurement, the space lacks dimensional homogeneity, so the Euclidian concept of geometrical distance does not apply.

We shall investigate the above questions later in the book. Suffice it here to say that the possibility of two different concepts of value existing side by side, such as value in use and value in exchange, is an idea that microeco-nomic theory does not allow and its founders were proud of doing away with. The national accounts, however, are not only capable of but are also compelled to employ more than one system of values. They may have some-thing to add to, as well as drawing from, the knowledge that was exposed intuitively, albeit less scientifically, in the earlier literature.

Going back to the theory that prevailed before the marginalist revolution means exhuming the classical theory of value. As it has been under the ground for a long time, its remains may not look appealing, and a lot of imagination and controversial interpretation will be required to piece them together.

The principle advantage of classical value theory is that it depicts value largely as a social relationship determined by continuous reproduction and social norms of consumption. Classical economists could not conceive of value existing without money, and the idea that commodities were not homogeneous and prices were highly variable was the norm in this pre-industrial world.

We do not intend to prove that classical theory is right and microeconomic theory is wrong, just to raise a grain of doubt about some of the charges for which classical theory was hanged in the rise to power of the marginalist revolution. With the hindsight gleaned from today's national accounts, arguments that seemed convincing then have lost some of their force today. Also, the fact that Marx is counted among the classical theorists shall not deter us, even if he is the alleged father of the material product system of accounts and this has been given the sack by the SNA in the course of globalisation. Remember that our aim here is to entertain rather than reveal the truth, although the two are not necessarily incompatible.

The national accountant may find our presentation of the accounts, by their very abstraction, oversimplistic and their interpretation not in accordance with his or her own, while discerning no advantage in loading them with what appears to be an unnecessary complex theory of value. For the economist, who rarely probes into the national accounts anyway, the conceptual finesses of the accounts will appear as statistical noise or a cloud of smoke that blurs an otherwise lucid theory without adding anything essential to the understanding of economic behaviour. And that a theory of value that so beautifully convinced generations of economists should be challenged by statisticians is likely to be regarded by economists as a sign of disobedience, if not a lack of knowledge, rather than as a contribution to their own work. But if theory is said to perform the task of setting up hypotheses – that is, conditional statements linking possible premises to necessary consequences – it is up to the statistical operation to determine whether these statements are facts. If the concepts within which the theory is set are other than those which can be measured in a capitalist economy, the statements have little meaning. It is true that compliance between theory and measurement has always been called for, but this has been a one-way exhortation: statisticians, please follow the right road, do what theory tells you and what you have learned at school! The entertaining point is to reverse the imperative and to assume that statisticians know what they are doings and which concept of value rules our economies (because they measure it), while the theory of value is still roaming about in a pre-accounting world, needing some adjustment to modern empirical techniques.

Since this book is meant to traverse the path from national accounts to the theory of value, its structure came naturally. It begins with a nutshell presentation of national accounts, reducing the rules and recommendations of national accounting to their basic principles and axioms (Chapter 2). The first principle in a statistical enterprise is that the object of observation must be defined. What is it that is to be measured by means of national accounts statistics? Naturally it is the values transacted between the units of an economy. What precisely these transactions are is the first topic to be investigated, and this will also reveal something about the values, being transacted. Chapter 3 turns to the economic agents who run the economy and transmit their value figures to the economic institutions of a society. Since it is impossible to compile individual reports for each institutional unit, it is necessary to classify and aggregate them in the process of data collection. This has repercussions on their meaning. From the data on value transactions between economic institutions the accountant derives information on the value of the production of the economy as a whole, that is, its gross domestic product (GDP). This presupposes the prior definition of a production boundary, and as this is a controversial issue some pages need to be devoted to unravelling the arguments. Some of the difficulties are due to the unreasonable application of the microeconomic theory of production to the macro level, and would disappear if a truly macroeconomic theory were applied.

The national accounts also measure income. Here the national accounts are more easily interpreted by means of the classical theory of value than by its microeconomic successor. In the national accounts, national income derives solely from national production. Asset increases due to holding gains – that is, pure exchange mechanisms – lie outside the income accounts. This is a Smithian rather than a Walrasian income concept. One may hold the view, of course, that the income concept is wrong for this very reason. But it is more entertaining to look at it the other way, and to ask why national accountants pursue the classical concept.

Putting together transactions and institutions is principally done in nominal terms. For the period and the territory under consideration there is assumed to exist a common, homogeneous unit of accounting carrying one and the same value through all transactions. But over more than one period of time and for other territories this assumption is counterfactual. We need to do accounting in real terms to enable comparisons of economic variables over and through these elementary categories of human perception.

This issue defeats microeconomic theory, which has never managed to provide a satisfactory recommendation for this objective of measurement, and the issue has thus been dubbed a 'problem'. This problem is twofold and relates to statistical aggregation in a given classification. The index number problem addresses heterogeneity between groups or classes (see Chapter 4) and the problem of quality change (Chapter 5) concerns heterogeneity within a class, both of which are familiar to statistical specialists in price measurement but hardly recognised by the generalists of value theory. It will be entertaining to show that these so-called problems have been effectively solved by the procedures used since the adoption of the 1993 SNA, if one relaxes certain of the normative assumptions that constitute microeconomic value theory.

Having presented the frame work of the national accounts in Chapters 2 to 5 we then discuss the insights gained into value theory. To pave the way it is necessary to identify the differences that exist between the two theories. We do this by juxtaposing the national accounting axioms with the axioms of microeconomic value theory, a standard representation of which has been achieved by Debreu. The juxtaposition of the two sets of axioms (Chapter 6) will help clear the path to a truly macro (that is, aggregate) theory of value. This goal can be approached in two ways. One is to apply the concept of value directly to the national accounts when interpreting their results. This seems a strange suggestion given that all national accounting figures are in values. But this simple fact has not really been recognised in some of the standard interpretations, especially in connection with the new concern of ecological economics (Chapter 7). The other way is by means of the classical theory of value. While it certainly cannot be said that the classical theory holds the entire key, it contains many elements of thinking that are macro-economic in nature, and thus provides fruit for a modern national account-ing value theory.

There is probably no single reader with a professional interest in all chap-ters. The enlightened reader will choose which to read and which to skip over. National accountants may occupy themselves with Chapters 2 and 3, price statisticians with Chapters 4 and 5, and value theorists with Chapters 6 to 8. Each will find ample material for debate. But the debate lies not within each field, but between them. The theory defended in each field cannot be justified by arguments from within that field, although these must at least be plausible, but from the interconnecting fields as this is an interdisciplinary venture. And the presentation in this introduction of two quotes from Adam Smith was not an arbitrary choice. Adam Smith stood for unity of observa-tion and reasoning, and in spite of the progress that has been made since his time in terms of thinking and methods his problems are still ours, as is his inspiration in dealing with them.

This book has not been written in one stroke. Given the complexity of the subject matter it seemed advisable to pick out particular chapters and pub-lish the material in separate articles in advance in order to develop and test the ideas. The feedback from these exercises has been incorporated here. I am grateful to Anne Harrison who read and criticised the whole book. Her comments led to major improvements in the arrangement and ordering of the text. Keith Povey did an excellent job in copy-editing, assuring accessibility not only to the professional but also to the layman in the field. My greatest recognition goes to Nancy and Richard Ruggles, on the one hand, and András Bródy, on the other, from whom I not only learnt the fundamentals of what is presented here, but whose continuous interest and support of this endeavour over many years helped to overcome all obstacles.

We close this introduction with an allegory. It was half a century ago that Richard Stone drew up his first design for the new national accounts. He was not concerned with the theory of value, taking it for granted in its textbook form. Piero Sraffa, at the same time but independently, developed his value theory of the production of commodities by means of commodities, not caring about its measurement and perhaps taking it for granted. Both were working in Cambridge, one on the left bank of the River Cam, at the Department of Applied Economics, the other on its right, at Trinity College. Perhaps the time has now come to try to bridge the Cam.

Part I
Nominal Accounts

2
Transactions and Their Economic Functions

This is the first of four chapters on the principles of national accounting, beginning with the definition of an economy. After briefly outlining what is meant by the measurement of economic value, the transactor/transaction principle is exposed as the fundamental rule for determining the data for national accounts. A hierarchical system of terms is constructed, detailing the transaction concept and clarifying its classification criteria. Then the concept of transformation is brought in as a complement to transactions needed for determining the value of production and consumption. A digression into the history of the debate on the transaction concept completes the chapter.

Basic concepts and principles

Value as a category of statistical measurement

As mentioned in the Introduction, this book is devoted to explaining the hypothesis that the national accounts imply a theory of value, and that this theory is different from the traditional microeconomic model. Microeconomic theory is generally taught but is not operational, while the national accounts theory of value is operational but not taught. More precisely, merely to say that value is the equilibrium price of a competitive economy gives no indication of how to measure this value, while the values statistically measured by means of the System of National Accounts (SNA) imply a different theory, one which needs to be made explicit in order to be understood. What is meant by such terms as 'operational' or 'statistical measurement'? Can values be measured at all?

The historical root of this question is contained in the dichotomy of a 'subjective' as offered to an 'objective' value concept, the first having been introduced by the so-called 'marginalist' school over a hundred years ago (Jevons, Walras, Menger) and the second by its predecessor, the classical school (Smith, Ricardo, Marx). Today's term is not 'subjective value', but 'individual preferences'. The important message of the microeconomic model is that competitive markets are a means of transforming subjective, and hence unknown, values into an objective market price. But this tells us nothing about how that price is measured. It is just the application of a mathematical fixed point theorem to an economic mechanism. If we want to know how to measure prices, we must study the theory and practice of national accounts in general and of price statistics in particular.

For the national accounts the task is not to determine the conditions under which subjective preferences can be transformed into an objective price, but, more trivially, the conditions under which an individual, or a statistician, for that matter, knows that a price is objective. Imagine that A and B exchange a horse and a cow, C and D exchange a shirt and a hat, and E and F exchange some items of food. How can they know or guarantee that their trade is equivalent? The answer can be found on the first pages of our economics textbooks: it is money that provides this guarantee. However, our textbooks are not precise on the issue. They usually point out that money facilitates exchange, and thus helps to establish markets. But they fail to say that money is also a condition of the existence of an objective and measurable concept of value. Somehow this tends to be forgotten by textbook authors when they turn from general economics to the theory of the consumer. The circulation of a well-defined currency as a means of payment, as an abstract commodity that has no use value in itself, is the precondition for making economic value an observable category. It is well known that this condition implies the use of money as a store of value and an accounting unit – functions that only an objective measure of value can perform. Hence it is logical that the political entity of a currency area constitutes what the macroeconomic theory of value defines as an economy. Let us state this as the first principle of national accounts:

- Proposition 1.1: an *economy* is the set of value transactions between economic units in a currency area.

According to this proposition the elementary object of observation in national accounts statistics is the transaction of value between economic agents, and the national accounts construct an image of the economy by collecting and classifying these transactions. This is an objective value concept in that it abstracts from any individual condition under which such transactions may occur, treating these as mere statistical aberrations from the underlying average.

But if an objective value concept seems so appropriate to macroeconomics, why was it defeated by microeconomic theory? We believe this was partly a result of insufficient economic development. At the time of the classical theorists, economic institutions were not yet fully developed. Currencies, in particular, had not yet grown out of their commodity shell.

They were precious metals that tended to reflect supply and demand in their own markets rather than the markets for other commodities. In perceiving an abstract yet generally accepted concept of value the classical theorists were ahead of their time. Reducing this concept to something more concrete – for example labour, as in our beaver and deer story in the Introduction – helped to illustrate the objectivity of the concept but was insufficient in terms of explicative power and range of application. Today, with a fully developed currency system, there is no question that economic value is measured precisely by currency and nothing else, no matter what the individual preferences behind it may be. No one will deny that a euro, a pound sterling or a dollar incorporate the same value under all conditions and for all purposes in their respective domains.

This does not mean, however, that modern monetary institutions have found the 'absolute measure of value' that so preoccupied the classical economists, Ricardo in particular. On the contrary, there is no such absolute measure – at the macro level everything in an economy is endogenous, including the measure of value. What we do have is acceptance by the world's banking institutions of the consumer price index as the measure of value of money. This is definitely not an invariant measure, as we shall discuss extensively in later chapters. Here, in order to keep the analysis simple and to proceed in an orderly way, we shall deal only with nominal values and ignore their eventual transformation into real ones. This conforms to the practice of national accounting, where in general nominal values are measured before prices and volumes.

We have stated rather bluntly that an economy is the set of value transactions in a currency area. This simple statement assumes we know what is meant by 'transaction', but in fact it will take the entire chapter clearly to analyse the value transaction concept of national accounts in a satisfactory way. The purpose of the exercise is to define concepts in such a way that their logical relationship is exposed. And even if the reader is not convinced of the outcome, following the trial may be entertaining.

The transactor/transaction principle of value realisation

If we assume that a currency area defines an economy, what objects should we collect in the corresponding accounts? The collected data should refer to economic life. The statistics should be comprehensive, bearing the trace of each and every event of economic relevance. Also, in order to be informative the statistics must compress information. The traces of economic events must lend themselves to aggregation. That is, they must be additive. Finally, in order to be economically meaningful they must express something about value. All these requirements are combined in a principle that is well known in the national accounts: the transactor/transaction principle, whereby observations of value transactions between the economic units of a country provide the principle data for the national accounts. The transactor/transaction principle conforms to business accounting, which lies at the heart of national accounting, not only as its historical and theoretical predecessor but also as the mechanism that generates the required data for the national accounts (SNA, 1993, para. 1.58). The transactor/transaction principle ensures that the accounts are objective. It forbids the accountants to set up accounts as they please, but requires them to work as statisticians. Values should be observed, not assumed by accountants.

In order to specify the nature of these data it is natural to begin with business accounts. Each business manages a certain amount of capital, the composition and development of which are controlled by means of a balance sheet showing the assets and liabilities of the business (Figure 2.1).

In the following we shall develop the concept of value transaction from the basic principles of a business account. This approach has been followed by Alfred Stobbe (1994), one of the most influential writers on national accounts in Germany. It combines an axiomatic hierarchy of concepts with parsimonious use of criteria to define them, a presentation that enables a comparison to be made between national accounts and value theory.

We begin by explaining the balance sheet shown in Figure 2.1, which provides information on the property worth of an economic unit, juxtaposing assets and liabilities. Assets are entities that function as a store of value (SNA, 1993, para. 13.12). There are two types of asset: those which are matched by an equal liability of another economic unit and those which are not.[1] The first are called financial assets, the second non-financial assets. Within the second category, those assets which are produced are again

Assets	Liabilities
Non-financial assets	Liabilities
Produced	
Non-produced	
Financial assets	
Currency and deposits	
Securities	
	Net worth

Figure 2.1   SNA balance sheet
Source: SNA (1993), Table 2.1 and annex to Chapter XIII.

distinguished from those which are not. Financial assets – which are not produced, of course, although claims are 'created', – are divided into liquid assets (currency and deposits) and non-liquid assets (securities), the first being characterised by their ability to act as a generally accepted means of payment. They are what the economist calls money. Net worth is the balance of the account, as distinct from gross worth, which is the sum of all assets. Net worth thus equals gross worth minus all liabilities. These categories are taken as given in a capitalist economy and reflect the economic organisation of the legal institution of property. On this institutional basis we can define (1) an economic event and (2) a value transaction.

- Definition 2.1: an *economic event* is any event that affects the property worth of an economic unit, as recorded on its balance sheet.

The interpretation of this definition is as follows. An economic unit acts and reacts to all kinds of events in its life, and is at one and the same time an economic unit, a social unit, a technical unit and an historical and cultural unit, a company for example. Not all its actions and behaviour are economic in nature, but those which are affect the worth of the property of the unit by changing an asset or a liability, or both. One might argue that there is hardly any major event that does not have this effect. But here the detached point of view of the statistician comes in: one looks at events affecting property inasmuch as this is recorded on the balance sheet of the unit. The balance sheet is the observable worth. Questions about the extent to which the balance sheet reflects actual or true worth are ignored in the interest of observability.

For the national accounts this has two consequences. First, it is not the national accountant who decides what should appear on the balance sheet of a business; on the contrary, it is the business accountant's data that provides the raw material for the national accountant. Second, the precise conditions under which an event should be recorded on a business balance sheet are legally and institutionally defined. They vary between countries, sometimes even within a country, so that the national accountant has a task of her or his own. In order to make the observed data homogeneous she or he must adjust the data, even during the early stage of collection, in order to make them comparable. Preparing for comparability means ridding the data of any effects that are accidental or not essential to the central characteristics of the envisaged accounting concept. The conflict between the two principles – passive recording and active adjusting – leads to a limit of application. National accounting can only be performed in a meaningful way if the differences in the rules of keeping balance sheets are small compared with the quantitative effects that are measured by means of them. If balance sheets were drawn up at the discretion of each unit, with the assent of its individual stakeholders but without any general or legal framework, this would not support the construction of national accounts. The rigidity of the national accounts as a system of flows and balances is acceptable as an adequate picture of an economy inasmuch as commerce itself is conducted within an equally rigid system of legal and social constraints that can be mirrored in homogeneous accounts.

- Definition 2.2: a *value transaction*, or transaction in the strict sense, is the creation between two economic units of a paired and equal claim and liability for payment in money.

This definition refers to exchanges between economic units that affect the property worth of the units, as reflected in the term 'transaction'. The content of the transaction is also defined. Valuable objects may pass between economic units, and this is often called a transaction 'in kind.' But properly speaking this is not correct. For in a money economy it is only money that functions as an objective measure of value, and any other valuable object will in all probability be valued differently by the two economic agents. This is why it is only when a transaction occurs in money – the normal means of exchange in a capitalist economy – one can say the value has been 'realised'. It has been transformed into a general, abstract form that is suitable as a means of payment for any other good. The passage of money is a necessary condition for the realisation of economic value.

This definition is a matter of social convention, of course, but it is embodied in the financial system of a country which cannot easily be changed. This is why we insist that value in money is different from value in kind. The denomination of the means of payment is not just a numéraire but a constituent element of value.

There are other events that affect property worth. If a claim is created, for example, one also needs to know how it is discharged. This is an economic event, in the sense defined above, and it is called payment. Value transactions in terms of claims and liabilities are paid for money transactions. Both belong together, the creation of the claim and its discharge. They are related through credit. Only one of them needs to be observed as a value measurement.

Other events that affect the property worth of an economic unit may occur within that unit alone, independently of other units:

- Definition 2.3: a *value transformation* is an economic event that affects the property worth of a unit internally.

Put briefly, value transactions that involve the acquisition of assets and liabilities are not the only events that affect the property worth of an economic unit. Produced assets are used up in production, and then reproduced; non-produced assets, be they financial or non-financial, are not used up but are only subject to 'other changes' in volume or price, as the SNA calls them, such as catastrophic losses or collapsing markets. Employing a term introduced by Gorter (1988) we call these events 'intransitive' and describe them as value transformations (Müller, 1984).

By way of example, take the sale of a commodity. This creates an equal claim and liability between seller and buyer. It is transaction of value, it is a transitive event in that value passes from one unit, the debtor, to another, the creditor. The idea of a passage of value is allowed because the claim created by one unit is equal to the liability incurred by the other. Were the entries in the two accounts not equal there could be no passage as value would be lost or added on the way. In contrast the production of a commodity is an intransitive event that affects only the internal circulation of the capital of the producing unit, transforming one type of asset, an input, into another, output.

It so happens that value transactions between units and value transformations within units are intrinsically linked to one another. If there were no transactions, production and consumption would be confined to individual economic units and there would be no market economy. If there were no production and use of products, goods could be exchanged but prices would have no continuity in time and would be purely speculative in character. Markets would be highly unstable. A modern economy is characterised by a highly developed division of production on the one hand and well-functioning markets and property rules on the other. Together they provide the ingredients for concept of economic value.

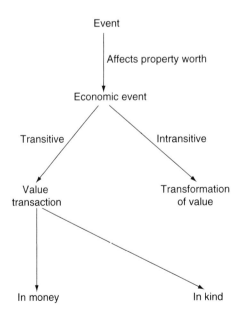

Figure 2.2 The hierarchy of accounting concepts

Figure 2.2 summarises the definitions provided in this section. Of all 'events' constituting the world[2], those that affect property worth are called economic. These too are divided into two categories, distinguished by being either transitive or intransitive – the first are called transactions, the second value transformations. Transactions are in turn divided into monetary transactions and those in kind. It must be said that the SNA is not overly rigorous in defining these terms because 'transactions take so many forms that . . . any general definition is inevitably rather imprecise' (SNA, 1993, para. 3.15). But the SNA has a different purpose from the one we have here. We shall return to this later.

What is the purpose of the axiomatic presentation here? We are searching for a relationship between the national accounts and the theory of value, and as the theory of value is presented in axiomatic form, for the sake of clarity and comparability we must present the national accounts in the same abstract way. The axiomatic presentation gives them a certain clarity, and although it may at first be difficult to accept, because of its lack of concreteness, it helps to construct a link to the theory of value.

The theory of pure transactions

Classifying transactions

We beg the reader not to rush ahead, but to remain patient. National accounts are geared to the purpose of measuring domestic product, and domestic product cannot be compiled from pure transactions alone. But since the figure has to be expressed as a monetary value and this value is realised only in transactions we must ensure that their measurement comes out correctly. The transaction must be entered into the accounts of two different economic units at the same time and in an equal amount. This is the condition under which we speak of a 'passage' of value between the two units, on the basis of which is constructed the concept of a circuit of value through the economy. We take this postulate even more seriously than does the SNA. While the SNA says that 'each economic flow or stock should be measured identically for both parties involved' (SNA, 1993, para. 2.16), we stress that equality should not only be incorporated into the rules of national accounting, where it can always be achieved at will, but should also be a criterion in respect of the data. Value is realised as an objective fact only when it is registered in an equal amount in the accounts of two units. And only under this premise does the accounting rule of equality make sense as a rule of data treatment.

The basis of registration of an equal value in the accounts of owners is either a civil contract or a public law. The SNA makes 'mutual agreement' a criterion, but then has trouble arguing for the inclusion of payments that are in agreement but are not 'voluntary' (ibid., para. 3.14). It is easier to argue the other way round: that a claim and liability come into existence through force of law, so that on the basis of voluntary, and yet legally defined contracts one can sue or be sued in court. A purely voluntary act outside the legal framework creates no claim to any property. When a transaction is entered into the accounts of the parties to the transaction, value has been 'realised'. It has switched in quality from a planning variable *ex ante*, which need not necessarily be consistent with values of other units, to a fact, a variable *ex post*, where accounting constraints are binding.

Further understanding of how value comes into existence as an observable fact can be gained by studying the classification of transactions engraved in the national accounts. Figure 2.3 provides an overview, extending Figure 2.2 downwards and beginning with the transaction concept. While the classification is well known, our presentation here is aimed at identifying the criteria that determine the distinctions between the categories. Transactions fulfil economic functions, and it will be interesting to see whether the assignment of these functions is a matter of judgement or is coupled to formal criteria embodied in the rules of the economy itself. This is what we try in the following. We classify transactions according to the manner in which they affect the different assets defined in Figure 2.1.

Figure 2.3 is supported by the following definitions:

- Definition 2.4: a transaction is called *economic* if it affects net financial worth.
- Definition 2.5: a transaction is called *financial* if it does not affect net financial worth.

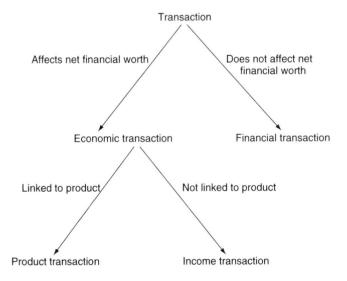

Figure 2.3 Classification of monetary value transactions

In this book the balance of financial claims and liabilities is called 'net financial worth'. This concept is not mentioned in the European system of accounts (SNA), but the ESA refers to it as a memorandum item of 'net financial assets' (ESA, 1995, para. 7.67). It makes sense to define transactions according to whether they affect or do not affect this balance. The reason why net financial worth is chosen here as the criterion of distinction – instead of net worth, the more commonly used balance – is the transaction principle. Net worth can be affected by events other than transactions, such as use in production, while net financial worth balances transactions only.

If the balance of claims and liabilities is affected, a transaction may be called 'economic' (Stobbe, 1994). Economic transactions include product transactions and income transactions of both which affect the balance of claims and liabilities. Unlike the SNA, we prefer the term economic transactions to non-financial transactions as the latter says less. Unlike financial transactions, product transactions and income – or, as they are also called – distributive transactions determine national product and income, and this important feature can be expressed by combining them into the category 'economic transactions'. Financial transactions, on the other hand, are non-economic in the sense that they play no role in the measurement of production in the accounts.

- Definition 2.6: a *product transaction* creates a claim that is linked to the delivery of a product.
- Definition 2.7: an *income transaction* creates a claim – without being linked to a product.

Let us illustrate the criteria by means of three examples: a commodity sale, a wage disbursement, and the purchase of a credit. Figure 2.4 demonstrates the different balance effects. The sale of a commodity, be it produced or not, affects property in two ways: it diminishes the stock of goods and increases the stock of receivable claims. The two values are usually unequal because the sale brings a profit, which is part of the value of the claim against the buyer, while the stock of goods is diminished by the value of the good to the seller, which is the cost. The stock held by the purchaser (not shown in the figure) is increased by the same good, but valued at the purchasing price. The good has two values in this event. This is why, when measuring the value of the contracted business, we concentrate on the monetary event; and since a sale – by creating a claim – increases the net financial worth of the seller (+60), and reduces the net financial worth of the buyer, this is an economic transaction by definition. It is called economic because the complementary entry in the account is not another financial asset but a product. The value of the product is imputed from the monetary observation. We say the product is valued at market price.

(a) Sale of a commodity

Asset changes		Liability changes	
Non-financial assets	−50	Liabilities	
Financial assets	+60		
		Net worth	+10
		Net financial worth	+60

(b) Disbursement of a wage or interest

Asset changes		Liability changes	
Non-financial assets		Liabilities	+30
Financial assets			
		Net worth	−30
		Net financial worth	−30

(c) Raising a loan

Asset changes		Liability changes	
Non-financial assets		Liabilities	+100
Financial assets			
Deposits	+100		
Securities		Net worth	0
		Net financial worth	0

Figure 2.4 The effect of different transactions on property

Financial transactions leave net financial worth intact, because for each claim there is a corresponding and equal liability on the same unit.[3] Economic transactions, however, transcend the narrow realm of finance, coupling it to real assets and production inputs. They build a bridge between the mechanism of exchange, measuring value, and the resources that generate it: labour and nature. Net financial worth is the stock variable corresponding to the flow variable of financial deficit, in the sense that the financial deficit or surplus of a unit equals the change in its net financial worth. Thus one can also differentiate between transactions by saying that economic transactions affect financial deficit, while financial transactions do not. The European issue of government deficit has to do with this distinction, and it has brought to light some interesting questions of detail, which we leave aside.

Income transactions are different from product transactions in that their value is not proportionate to an amount of product in return. Labour may be paid in proportion to its being delivered (for example by the hour, or even by the piece), but labour is not a product, hence wages are not a product transaction. Payment for capital goods is a product transaction, of course, but the interest paid on credit is not as credit is not produced. This is complicated by the fact that intermediate financial institutions organise the credit system of an economy. Thus interest transactions may contain a service component, but for the sake of clarity we shall ignore this. Pure credit is simply the creation of a claim counterbalanced by a liability. The interest on it is an income transaction. Income transactions are the means through which the distribution of products is effected, hence their official name, 'distributive transactions'.

In terms of value theory, income transactions are interesting because the claim arises when the payment falls due. A salary may be paid at the beginning of the working period or at its end. The liability of the employer arises on the day of payment, as set down in the labour contract. The proof of this is that liabilities for work performed for employers are not found on commercial balance sheets. An employee can sue only for a claim that has fallen due, not for the work he or she has done. Likewise for interest – a bank cannot sue a company for payment of interest if the payment is not due by contract, even if the money lent has already been spent on a new machine and profit has been made with it.

Terminology in the manuals of national accounting

For those who cherish the national accounts a word of explanation is in order in respect of comparing our abstract and formal criteria for classifying transactions with the definitions standardised in the SNA or ESA. A manual or a handbook has a different purpose than a pure theory, and this distinction must be kept in mind when the two texts are compared. According to the ESA:

> A transaction is an economic flow that is an interaction between institutional units by mutual agreement or an action within an institutional unit that it is useful to treat as a transaction, often because the unit is operating in two different capacities.
>
> (ESA, 1995, para. 1.33)

Obviously this definition of transaction is broader than ours. We would call only the first part of the ESA definition that is the interaction between economic units' a transaction; the second part ('as action within an institutional unit') we see as a value transformation. The difference in definition is partly due to our different usage of the term transaction at the beginning. In definition 2.2 a value transaction is presented an economic event. It occurs in the economy, irrespective of whether or not it is recorded in the national accounts. In the ESA, as well as in the SNA and the national accounts literature in general, transaction is also understood as an entry in the accounts, an accounting 'operation' as the French say. Part of the confusion about the definition of transaction is due to there being insufficient distinction between two levels of action: action in the economy (event) and action in the accounts (registration). This is why we began our taxonomy with the initial event. The ESA, apparently, uses the term 'flow' to denote the same thing: 'Flows reflect the creation, transformation, exchange, transfer or extinction of economic value. They involve changes in the value of an institutional unit's assets or liabilities. ' (ibid., para. 1.32). Thus while there is a difference in terminology, it does not lie at the conceptual level. In principle the categories of economic phenomena defined here are the same as in the manuals.

Another issue has to do with what is normally treated under the heading 'time of recording'. The SNA discusses three of those times: cash basis, due for payment, and accrual accounting (SNA, 1993, paras 3.92–6). This implies that there is just one value transaction which can be observed at different stages of its passage from the debtor to the creditor. Actually this is not so – all these 'times' are different events in their own right, but in many instances of ordinary business life they hang together, so that one calls them one 'transaction'. In theory we must be more scrupulous.

Recording on a cash basis means that one looks at payments for liabilities. This is tantamount to extinguishing an existing claim and liability pair. In our terminology this is not a transaction, it is payment for a transaction. And it is common knowledge that not all liabilities are paid. Thus there is a discrepancy between actual values, not only in theory but also in practice. Equilibrium values of exchange refer to the claim and liability when they arise, not their eventual payment or non-payment. Of course in some areas of the economy data are only recorded on a cash basis. In such cases, government statistics for example, there must be an adjustment. What we argue is that payment for a transaction is often related to, but not conceptually identical to, the creation of an equal claim and liability, which is the actual value transaction.

The difference between 'cash basis' and 'due for payment basis' is that in one case the liability is extinguished and in the other it is created, that is, from now on a credit is afforded to the debtor. Timing at 'payment due' therefore equals the value of the original transaction 'at accrual'. For some transactions particularly income transactions, the time of falling due equals the time the claim arises. The claim for wages comes into existence when they fall due, likewise for interest, social security and other social payments.

The SNA, after some discussion, opted for accrual accounting. Unfortunately accrual means a lot of different things: 'Accrual accounting records flows at the time economic value is created, transformed, exchanged, transferred or extinguished' (SNA, 1993, para. 3.94). If this were taken seriously we would have a lot of incompatible values in the national accounts. The collection of items in the quotation is not well-reflected but it contains a certain truth. Value actually grows through the physical process of transformation, but it is measured through exchange, a legal process of contracting, and between the two there is a relationship but no identity. The statement tells us that pure transactions in the sense of our definitions are not enough to construct meaningful national accounts. They reflect just the surface of the economy, and to look beneath the surface and probe into the processes of production and the generation of income are purposes of accounting. This brings in a new feature of the economic world – duality.

The duality of economic events and its reflection in the operations of accounting

The analytical distinction

In our terminology value transactions are distinguished from value transformations, the first being a transitive and the second an intransitive economic event (Figure 2.2). But if the two are conceptually distinct, in reality they are intrinsically connected because there is no production without exchange, and *vice versa*. The duality of value transaction and value transformation must be accounted for if the property worth of an economic unit is to be comprehensively controlled. Correspondingly, two kinds of operation are possible in the accounts. One is the simple registration of a figure, such as the registration of a transaction at its market price. The other is a calculation, or technically speaking, 'an imputation' of value, to follow up the internal processes of a business. The figure entered into the accounts for the consumption of fixed capital is a case in point, but even the ordinary output figure – being composed of sales, a transaction and a net increase in stock, which is an intransitive event – makes use of such an imputation.

The critical point in respect of the duality of economic events is that the transformation of assets through production and consumption is the essential origin of value, but in itself it is not observable. Value is realised, as the businessman says, in exchange, in transactions. Transactions are thus statistical observations that can be entered into the accounts directly, while the value of transformations can only be inferred from the data on transactions on the basis of some accounting rule (imputation). This duality of accounting operations is deeply imbedded in the organisation of the economic process and has given rise to ardent practical and theoretical dispute in the national accounts profession.

	Payables	Receivables
Product transactions		Sales 90
Income transactions	Wages 100	
Financial transactions		Loans 10
	100	100

Figure 2.5   Pure transaction account of a producing unit

At this stage it is sufficient to demonstrate the duality of structure embedded in the accounts by means of a simple example (Figure 2.5). Let claims of 90 from product transactions be combined with incurred liabilities of 100 for income transactions, resulting in a deficit of 10, which in equilibrium is financed by the capital market. Figure 2.5 is a pure transaction account. The dotted lines indicate that each group of transactions gives rise to its own sub-account: the production account, the income account and the finance account, each of which are further subdivided and refined in the sytem of national accounts. These accounts can be closed by their own balance for analytical purposes, but obviously they are not economically complete. We have accounted for exchange, but not for production.

Accounting for production means that we not only recognise value flows between units, but also follow up the transformation that assets undergo within producing units. This internal capital circuit is captured by concepts such as cost and performance, where the currency is used as an accounting unit but without a direct link to outside transactions. The correct statement of these results is the goal of business accounting. Although this internal accounting uses money as the accounting unit, the values determined in this way are not objective in the sense that they can be compared across companies. It is well known that balance sheets mean different things in different businesses, even if there are legal and other rules to which they conform. A certain commodity may carry a different internal value in different companies, depending on its function within the internal production process. At the macro level this cannot be controlled. Nevertheless, by asking each business, or a representative sample, for a figure for their increase in stock of finished products and production of fixed assets for their own use one can obtain an average value figure that may be considered as fairly objective.

To put it more theoretically, it is common to refer to value as something that can be represented by any commodity, thus it seems permissable to visualise the economic circuit as the circulation of wheat, gold or labour or any other good. Actually this is not so. Once money is recognised as the carrier of value, its unitary value is equal for all uses, to the exclusion of all others. Obviously, each commodity varies in its money price. It carries a different value according to this price, and hence one cannot say that it has the same value wherever it shows up in the economy as this quality has been assigned to money, by definition. (We shall return to this problem in Chapter 5, where we discuss the quality problem of price observation.) This is the reason why transactions in kind are fuzzy values. They have been effected outside the market, so comparison is difficult and one cannot assume that the value of the delivered good is equal for the transactors.

It makes a difference, for example, whether a car that is offered to an employee has been bought or produced by the employer company. If a doctor accepts a 'payment in wine instead of money' (SNA, 1993, para. 3.39), this may indicate a scarcity of wine or of money. In the first case, wine is special and therefore preferred to money, in the second it is accepted because otherwise the doctor would not be paid at all. Valuation is quite different in each case. Fortunately the problem lies beyond the national accountant's reach. When business accounts are kept, these determine the valuation of transactions in kind, and when they are not, individual case studies must decide what monetary value to impute. This is the borderline of the market economy, and of the applicability of national accounts.

By adding to sales the value of increase in stocks and of capital formation on own account, one forms the SNA measure of production, called output. This is usually called a product transaction, or a transaction in goods and services. As we hope to have shown, this is acceptable for practical purposes. But in terms of theory, output is a complex aggregate, consisting of a registration of sales (pure transaction) and an imputation of internal worth increase. If this amount is 15, our example in Figure 2.5 changes into that shown in Figure 2.6.

The message of this account is quite different from that of its predecessor. In Figure 2.5, labour of 100 was expended to produce output worth 90. Taking account of internal accumulation, the same labour can now be shown to have produced an output worth 105. While in the pure transaction account it looks as though the credit mechanism financed wages, the correct imputation shows that in terms of finance this may have been the case, but in terms of economic resources it was not. The surplus labour was employed to increase assets.

This comparison of Figures 2.5 and 2.6 shows the necessity of making imputations in the national accounts with respect to the duality of economic events: the exchange of goods and services between units on the one hand, and their production and consumption within units on the other. Figure 2.6 is 'articulate', as the French say, in that it reveals the meaning of the transactions, something a pure transactions account (Figure 2.5) cannot do.[4] Figure 2.6 also shows the complexities that are introduced

	Uses	*Resources*
Product transactions		Sales 90
		Own account production 15
Income transactions	Wages 100	Savings 5
	Profit 5	
	Capital formation 15	
Financial transactions		Loans 10
	120	120

Figure 2.6   Value transaction and transformation account of a producing unit

through imputations in the accounts, especially when one looks at the balance of individual accounts. Such balances are formed for the purpose of arriving at certain analytical economic concepts. Thus the balance of the production account is the value added to the property of a unit through production, which would be equal to 105 in the example, the consumption of intermediate and capital goods being neglected. On the income account, value added is divided into wages of 100 and a profit of 5, the wages being disbursed and the profit being retained as savings. Together with net borrowing it finances capital formation of 15. The imputation of 15 on the production account requires balancing imputations on the income account, where the profit of 5 is balanced by 'saving', – the same figure under a different name – and on the capital account, which is merged here with the income account, showing a capital formation of 15. In this way the gross value of transactions increases from 100 in Figure 2.5 to 120 in Figure 2.6, where the 5 and the 15 are tautologically identical on both sides of the account.

One can see the seductive danger of extending the imputation technique to other areas outside the market. If a pure transaction account is inarticulate in its meaning this is matched by the opposite danger of overarticulation, of too many imputations that are uncontrolled. Housework is a case in point. At one point national accountants may have been inclined to yield to the demand of including housework in the accounts, but when empirical studies showed quantitative ranges of between 30 per cent and 60 per cent of GDP it became obvious that adding those amounts to the two sides of the account in identical values would render the transaction approach meaningless.

But first we shall carry the analysis of the production account to its conclusion. All the procedures and concepts used in Figure 2.6 are standard practice and not to be debated. But in order to demonstrate that there is a theory behind every imputation, let us look at undistributed profit. This is called income in the national accounts because it causes distributed income to add up to the value added derived from the production account. The underlying assumption is that income equals value added in the economic circuit. But this theory is open to debate.

Firstly, income is usually thought of as an inflow of liquidity, implying liberty in respect of deciding how to spend it or, in particular, whether it should be spent at all. Undistributed profit yields no liquidity. It has already been spent. It exists as an increase in produced assets. The savings rate of this 'income' is 100 per cent, by definition.

Secondly, profit may at times be negative, and when this is so national income comes out lower than household income, which is not sensible. Since income is theoretically derived from production in the national accounts and production can never be negative, the income derived from it cannot be so either. Also the nation as a whole can hardly have less income than its households as a sector. Negative income is reasonable as an exceptional circumstance for an individual business, but on the macroeconomic level it is a matter for the reconciliation account rather than the production account.

Thirdly, one may give a different interpretation of the residual, as part of a macroeconomic theory of value. If the economy is in equilibrium, implying that all three markets – product, labour and capital – are in mutual equilibrium, households' intention to save will match firms' desire to accumulate. This does not mean that businesses would work without profit, but that they would distribute all of their profit to their shareholders and let them decide about its use. A positive residual of undistributed profit would then indicate overaccumulation – that is, the producers would have invested more than households were willing to save – while a negative figure would mean undersaving of households.

In this interpretation we do not make inferences about disequilibrium from unobserved mathematical functions, but from observed variables. It must be added as a warning that in this particular case the national accounting figure of undistributed profit is often unreliable, being a residual of all accounts and of big number balances with all their errors being forwarded, so caution in its use is advised from a practical point of view. But even if our interpretation exercise is academic at the moment, it may help to prove that imputations of values in the accounts are not natural or self-evident but imply a certain perspective on the underlying economic process, and if not properly understood they simply mislead this very process.

The fact that income as an aggregate of pure value transactions (wages and distributed profits) between units is complementary to income as an accounting concept of internal transformation processes (value added) expresses the duality of economic events from a value theoretic point of view. National accounts in their full complexity provide for both, but this duality of a capitalist economy is not recognised in microeconomic theory, where physical and institutional phenomena are not differentiated, so on the basis of this theory it seems natural, if not necessary, to equate national income with national product. Further arguments on this issue will emerge when we study the institutional structure of the national accounts more closely in the next chapter.

The historical struggle between the concepts of transaction and transformation

In order to illustrate the practical relevance of the duality between production and exchange, let us recall part of the debate that accompanied the fourth revision of the SNA. When in 1981 the United Nations decided to review the existing system of accounts, dating from 1968, it did so in response to a decade of heated discussions. Economic growth, measured by gross domestic product, had come under attack world-wide as a meaningful goal of economic policy. Environmentalists pointed to the lack of concern about shrinking resources and the abatement of pollution. Feminists decried the omission of housework from the national accounts, while development economists called for a better analysis of subsistence production. Each political interest voiced its own demands. New concepts of GDP sprang up: 'regrettable necessities' should be subtracted; production beyond the market should be added; 'true' wealth or 'real' welfare measurement required that the value of leisure be included; quality of life should have a place in the national accounts; and so on. The advocated modifications of standard GDP all worked in more or less the same way. They demanded the imputing of new values to some traditional macroeconomic figure. Such imputations depended on the political or theoretical stance of the proponent, and were applied to a particular aggregate of the national accounts that seemed worthy of critique, mostly without concern for the implications for the rest of the accounting system. In the end it seemed that the national accounts were but a set of arbitrary conventions that could be remodelled at will by the statistician.

In light of this situation the UN Statistical Commission decided to review its system of accounts in order to simplify it, and to answer these challenges. A seminal paper by von Eck *et al.* (1983) showed the direction. In what amounted to a radical overhaul they proposed that the core system of accounts be purified of all imputations, and that the system be made more flexible by adding to the core building blocks of different areas, such as the environment, housework and so on, where specific imputations could be designed to express the meaning of the transactions for the particular area. Flexibility thus meant multidimensionality in terms of the required imputations.

The abolishment, or at least the critical evaluation, of imputed transactions in the national accounts had been voiced before by Nancy and Richard Ruggles in 1982 in an assessment of the US national income and products accounts. They recommended that in order to increase the transparency of accounting, imputed transactions should be shown separately so that the user might know and possibly change the imputations according to his or her own judgment.

The idea had its attractions, but it also met resistance. The debate climaxed at the 18th General Conference of the International Association for Research in Income and Wealth in Noordwijkerhout, Holland. Here the Dutch, who skilfully used their home advantage, were opposed by statisticians of a more functional bent. André Vanoli and the French school of thought spearheaded the counterargument, pointing out that a core of pure transactions would be void of analytical content. They insisted that the national accounts' primary purpose should be to measure the production of a country, agreeing that this would not necessarily imply the measurement of overall welfare. A core system had to include a workable notion of GDP and its subaggregates, and not just be a collection of payables and receivables running through each sector. It had to show the connection between national production and national income, with unambiguous figures for both. The transaction principle was not sufficient to construct meaningful national accounts. The accounts had to be 'articulate'.

Related to this controversy over accounting operations was another debate about the correct statistical unit for determining GDP. Some national accounts relied on the institutional unit, such as an enterprise (France, Germany), some on the establishment (Australia, Netherlands, UK, US, Canada). How could one ensure comparability? Each side had arguments in favour of their choice. Those who built their accounts upon institutions called attention to the fact that they had records for all types of transaction because any claim that arose was registered on the balance sheets of the institutional unit. Those whose accounts were based on establishments accepted that income and financial data might be missing, but that flows of goods and services, location and employment, in short all data that had to do with production, were more appropriately collected there. In the end the debate was decided by the statistical system that existed in each country and could not easily be overthrown by the SNA's recommendations. In terms of theory, the problem was solved by means of a cross-classification, as will be shown in Chapter 3.

In a similar way, the resolution of the conflict between a pure transaction core and a central system with specified imputations can be traced back to two principles, both of which are part of the national accounts. The transactor/transaction principle stresses the fact that national accounts are there to record statistical data. It ensures objectivity in the sense that the values shown in the accounts are not there as a result of subjective evaluation by some or other analyst, but as a statistical observation. The value revealed in a transaction is the only value that can be objectively and statistically observed for the purpose. On the other hand, in order to give the accounts meaning they must be articulate. Transactions must be classified by type, and some rearrangement and imputations relating the observed transactions to the underlying processes of production and consumption must be admitted. Observation and analysis are both desired aims of the national accounts, and as a result of the controversy at Noordwijkerhout they have been retrieved from under the piles of collected data and reconciled into an integrated system. The duality of economic events is reflected in the accounts by the dual principles of transaction recording on the one hand and the articulation of flows on the other.

In closing this chapter we recall Adam Smith's deer and beaver conundrum presented in the Introduction to this book. A production account that records values not when they are sold but when they are produced implicitly assumes that values are realised through production, not through sales. This idea carries even through to non-market production, where again value is recorded as having been realised when it has been produced. And the valuation of unsold products is at cost. If it takes twice the time to build a factory building than it does to build a building within an establishment the value of the first increase in fixed assets on own account is twice that of the second in the national accounts. Here Adam Smith appears around the value theoretic corner.

3
Institutions and Their Economic Activities

In this chapter we investigate the source of economic value: production. We show how national accounting relates the value transactions between economic agents to 'value added', as it is called internally, and how the duality of transaction and transformation is reflected in the duality of the enterprise as an institutional unit and the establishment as a functional unit of observation. This leads to the main theoretical question treated in this chapter: how to define production.

The units of observation

Institutional units: the economy and its sectors

Value theory is a theory about how value is created. And again we find that the answer is ambivalent in economics. For example, if we study the Edgeworth box, a typical microeconomic model, we arrive at the message that value is created through exchange. Not so in the national accounts. Here the necessary condition of value creation is production. Hence before we can know what value is, we must know what production is. As its definition relies on the concept of an institutional unit and its functional structure, this entity must be studied first. An institutional unit consists of capital employed in production, which may involve different activities by the people engaged in it. The logic of these concepts will now be developed step by step.

If the transactor/transaction principle circumscribes the field of data of the national accounts, as stated in the previous chapter, we must now address the question of who produces such data – in other words, who the transactors are who create the desired claims and liabilities in the system. At first sight the transactor/transaction principle seems obvious and almost trivial, merely another way of specifying who does what in an economy. However in skimming through the SNA (1993) one can find two types of economic agent: the institutional unit, and the production or functional unit. The first is aggregated to sectors and the second to industries, and each has its own classification. There is a dual structure in the national accounts concept of economic unit that corresponds to the dual character of economic events, as analysed in the previous chapter. This is new in value theory and adds to it another dimension of complexity. We begin by stating another proposition.

- Proposition 3.1: the *agents* of the economy are institutional units that hold and manage property. It is they who pay for and receive transactions.

This proposition must now be established. While we will follow the SNA, in doing so we will not suppress our own thoughts about value theoretic issues.

The institutional unit may be defined as an entity that is capable, in its own right, of owning assets, incurring liabilities and engaging in economic activities and transactions with other such entities (SNA, 1993, para. 3.2). There are thus three criteria – assets and liabilities, activities, and transactions – which must meet together in order to form an institutional unit. The corporate enterprise is a typical example. It owns assets and liabilities, engages in production, and sells to other enterprises. Actually the three criteria are not independent, there is a logical relationship between them. If a transaction is defined as the creation of a claim/liability pairing between two institutional units, this presupposes the existence of property rights. Thus the transactions that form the object of observation of the national accounts require the existence of transactors in the form of property holders. On the other hand, merely holding assets and liabilities does not constitute an active institutional unit – it must also engage in transactions, its capital must circulate. The first and third criteria are interrelated and refer to the institutional unit as a holder of legal rights.

Activity is an independent criterion – there are legal entities that pursue an economic activity, and others that do not. Post-office box and ghost firms are examples of the latter. Such firms are legally registered, have a postal address and even a balance sheet, but nobody works in them. Since the purpose of accounts is to establish a link between income and production in an economy, the SNA says that a unit must contain at least one entire establishment if it is to be called an institutional unit of the system (ibid., para. 2.47). Units without activity do not contribute to domestic product.

An economy is the set of all institutional units that are resident in the economic territory of a country (ibid., para. 2.22). The economic territory of a country is essentially the same as its geographical territory, but does not coincide exactly with it. Some qualifying additions and subtractions are made, for example embassies and military bases, because the decisive criterion is not a functional one (location) but – as it should be with institutions – a legal one. The economic territory is the territory over which the government has jurisdiction. This is logical, because the laws on assets and liabilities are the laws of a specific government. The concept of economic as opposed to geographical territory theoretically coincides with the use and validity of a certain currency based on the laws of one government. An economy is thus essentially defined by its currency area. It is not, as in the microeconomic model, that any number of agents with production functions and preferences form an economy, but that the nation is the only entity for which the concept of an economy with national accounts is operational, at least in theory, because national governance is the precondition for an economic circuit of value to function. It is the realm of macroeconomics proper.

An institutional unit is said to be a resident unit of a country when it engages for a year or more in economic activities on the economic territory of the country (ibid., para. 2.22). Again we find that activity is an essential element of the institutional unit. The theoretical concept of activity can be fruitfully translated into operational language by stating that in the resident unit there should be employment. But because the SNA definition has been adopted from the balance of payment manuals, at first sight it voices a more capital-oriented point of view: 'An institutional unit is said to have a centre of economic interest within a country when there exists some location – dwelling, place of production, or other premises – within the economic territory of the country on, or from, which it engages in economic activities and transactions on a significant scale' (ibid., para. 14.12). And 'the ownership of land and structures within the economic territory of a country is deemed to be sufficient in itself for the owner to have a centre of economic interest in the country' (ibid., para. 14.14). This seems to indicate that mere ownership suffices to make the owner an economic resident. But, somewhat obviously, it is also said that land and buildings can only be used for purposes of production in the country in which they are located. So in the end the activity point of view prevails. If the owner of the structures is a non-resident a notional institutional unit is created for the land and buildings in much the same way as a domestic quasi-corporation is separated from its owner. All this shows that production is the focus of analysis.

Sectors are mutually exclusive subsets of the set of institutions that form the economy:

- Non-financial institutions
- Financial institutions
- Government institutions
- Non-profit institutions serving households
- Households

The non-financial sector represents the bulk of the economy and generates most of the domestic product. Therefore in some countries, for example Germany, it is called the production sector, or the sector of productive enterprises, and the statistical tradition is followed of giving a separate descriptive label to the major categories in the classification (rather than just 'non-financial', which is like calling all animals 'non-humans'). The sector includes all corporations, private and public, and can be subdivided into national and foreign-controlled. Also included are quasi-corporations and institutions that do not work for profit but still produce for the market. They sell most or all of their output at economically significant prices, but are recognised by the financial authorities as non-profit organisations. Schools, universities and hospitals are examples.

The financial sector consists of institutions that engage in financial activities, such as banks (called 'depository corporations' in the SNA), insurance companies, pension funds, brokers and the central bank. Because financial mediation is inherently different from most other types of productive activity and because of the importance of financial mediation in the economy, financial institutions are distinguished from the other profit-making institutions at the first level of the sectoral system (ibid., para. 4.77). The distinction of financial institutions sheds a light on the production boundary implied in the system, as we will show later.

The government sector comprises non-profit governmental institutions such as the units run by central, state or local government, social security funds, and non-market, non-profit institutions that are controlled and mainly financed by the government. The remaining non-profit institutions fall into the 'non-profit institutions serving households' sector. Examples are professional societies, political parties, churches, clubs and so on.

Households are the fifth and last sector in this classification, but do not really obey its criteria. A household is defined as a small group of persons who pool their income and wealth, and collectively consume goods and services (ibid., para. 4.132). Property, the distinctive mark of the individualisation of an institutional unit – a unit that can sue and be sued – is rendered insignificant here, yielding to common accommodation as the distinctive criterion. In addition, consumption instead of productive activity is the characteristic functional feature. A household may be active in production or not, but all members consume. Hence the household sector stands apart from the institutional sectors in the strict sense. It is not a property unit containing at least one establishment. On the contrary, one may see it as a local activity unit (establishment) that includes at least one property unit (a person of full legal capacity), the opposite logical relationship to units of production. The opposition of households to institutional units indicates that there is something artificial about the distinction between groups of persons (households) and legal entities (institutional units), as established in the SNA. One might just as well treat households as establishments rather than institutional units. But actually households are not treated in their own right in the national accounts. The account of households serves mainly to close the economic circuit in a similar way as the rest-of-the-world account. A full analysis of households requires the extension of the national accounts to a social accounting matrix (SAM), which we leave aside here.

Figure 3.1 summarises the logic of sectoral classification. The five sectors distinguished in the SNA at the first level of aggregation are presented in italics. The household sector is complementary to the institutional units proper by virtue of its defining criteria. In the national accounts, institutional units combine property and production, as opposed to households, which consume in a common domestic location. Of the institutional units, those which produce under domestic civil law form the economy, as opposed to the rest of the world. Economic institutions are subdivided into profit and non-profit entities. The former could also be collectively called the capitalist sector, which makes it natural to separate the financial sector from the other sectors. Non-capitalist institutions are categorised as private or public. We thus arrive at the first level of the SNA classification. Figure 3.1 is designed to explain this classification in a theoretically stringent way.

Production units: industries and branches

A single enterprise, especially a large corporation, may simultaneously engage in numerous types of productive activity, there being virtually no upper limit to the size of such a (possibly international) corporation. For the macroeconomic and national analysis of production and its technology it is necessary, however, to work with aggregates of producers of a similar type, so if institutional units engage in diverse activities they must be broken down into smaller, more homogeneous, constituent parts. These are called establishments. An establishment is an enterprise, or part of an enterprise, that is

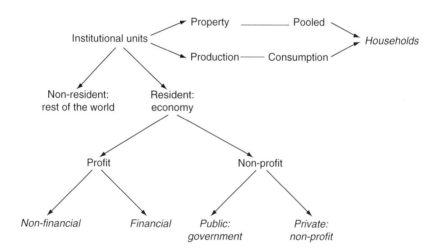

Figure 3.1   The logic of sectoral classification

situated in a single location and in which one activity, called the principal activity, accounts for most of the value added. If a secondary activity is important it should be treated as taking place in a separate establishment (ibid., para. 5.21). In contrast to the institutional unit, two functional criteria – activity and locality – define the production unit.

Actually it is not activity as such that matters but its type. Of course this differs between establishments in terms of output, materials and supplies consumed, the kind of equipment and labour employed and the techniques used. The limits of such activity are not easily defined. Given the modern division of labour in a firm it may be hard to draw demarcation lines and distinguish between production processes. For this reason the concept of establishment draws on locality as an additional criterion.[1]

An aggregate production account can thus be compiled in two ways: by focusing either on institutional units and their sectors, or on establishments and their industries. The distinction between and integration of the two types of statistical unit and their aggregation can be captured in a cross-classification of the entries of a production account ('dual sectoring'). Table 3.1 shows this for output.

The rows show the output of the economy by sector, while the columns show output by industry, as classified by the International Standard Industrial Classification (ISIC). Table 3.1 is a theoretical scheme and not many countries are able to compile it. Therefore the artificial numbers supplied in the SNA (ibid., Table 15.3) have been adapted here for the purpose of illustration.

Table 3.1 demonstrates that 'sector' and 'industry' are clearly not identical, but nor are they completely independent. For example column FE (financial services and education) has entries in all of the rows, which means that such services are supplied by all institutional sectors, while MC (manufacturing and construction) only has entries for non-financial institutions and house-

Table 3.1 Cross-classification of output by sector and industry (arbitrary money units)

Sector	Industry					
	AM	MC	TT	FE	NM	Total
Non-financial institutions	56	1243	191	230	33	1753
Financial institutions	–	–	–	102	–	102
Government institutions	–	–	–	76	364	440
Non-profit institutions	–	–	–	24	16	40
Households	57	809	100	189	114	1269
All sectors	113	2052	291	621	527	3604

Notes: AM = agriculture and mining; MC = manufacturing and construction; TT = trade and transport; FE = finance and education; NM = non-market output.

holds, the first supplying by far the larger share. Thus while enterprises and establishments are different in logic and conceptual content they are not fully disentangled in the economy, which is what one would expect – institutional structure reflects production structure to a certain degree.

Yet there are characteristic differences. The establishment is not a property holder in its own right. Consequently it does not engage in transactions of value in the strict sense. In contrast to the institutional unit, which registers all transactions, the establishment furnishes data only on aspects of production, such as output, intermediate input, employment and wages. An establishment does not have the shell of property rights around it that would allow it to participate in distributive or financial transactions. The establishment is a unit that comes closer to production, but this at the expense of information on the circulation of income and finance through the economy. The establishment is not able to establish a full set of accounts – this is the preserve of institutional units alone.

Taking yet another step away from the institutional context, one may abstract from locality and define the so-called homogeneous production unit on a purely activity basis. These units exist only in the abstract of aggregation. They are compiled by means of an input–output table and are mathematical averages over heterogeneous institutional data. The 1968 SNA provided a simple mathematical formula. If V is the matrix of output by type and industry, and U the corresponding matrix of inputs, the input structure of homogeneous production units, A, is given by the matrix operation:

$$A = UV^{-1} \tag{3.1}$$

The resulting aggregates, which are called branches in the French tradition, are then given by

$$X = A\hat{q} \tag{3.2}$$

where $\hat{q}$ is the diagonal matrix of output classified by type. The assumption behind this so-called commodity by commodity model is that each product corresponds exactly to one process of production in all institutions and establishments. Partly because of the lack of a statistical foundation, the 1993 SNA has not included this or any competing model in its recommendations.

Both units of production (the establishment and the homogeneous production unit) share in common the fact that the resulting aggregates – industries in the case of establishments, product branch in the case of homogeneous production units – disregard the institutional boundaries. They isolate productive activity from its institutional context, which disappears in the aggregation.

The reason for the duality of accounting concepts

Having established the dual character of the statistical units used in the national accounts, the need arises to explain and justify a structure that introduces an additional level of complexity into the system. Why are two types of statistical unit necessary? Van Bochove and van Tuinen (1986) provide one answer in their classical paper, written at the height of the discussion about the new SNA. There are two approaches to constructing national accounts: the institutional approach and the functional approach. The former stresses the formal and organisational features of transactors and transactions. As a consequence it remains close to the actual experience of economic agents and their observed data. The functional approach, in contrast, is analytical. It begins with an analysis of the function of transactions and looks behind their formal appearance to determine their economic nature. In fact it frequently concentrates on processes, products and similar categories rather than transactions. Consequently transactions that are quite different in formal appearance may be lumped together. In the functional approach transactors are defined in an indirect way, as the performers of processes. An example is the homogeneous production unit, constructed by means of the commodity X commodity transformation of industries into the branches referred to above (equation 3.1). The resulting figures do not correspond to directly observable transactions or institutions.

As explained in the previous chapter, national accounts need both approaches as each is insufficient on its own. Institutional units are necessary as the existing units of observation. They organise production and are in a position to answer questions about their value transactions with other units. However, if such transactions were recorded between sectors without reference to some functional analysis, the resulting aggregates would be meaningless. The functional approach supplies this analysis. It classifies transactions according to their function – goods and services, distributive, financial, to name only the first level of classification – and collects them on the corresponding accounts. In order to do so it makes use of attributions and imputations, which distort the actual transactions but render the accounts articulate in terms of economic analysis.

Observation of facts and articulation of meaning are the two principles upon which the national accounts are built, and this is the reason for the duality of statistical units. The accounts construct a path from the observable but functionally complex institutional unit to the abstract, homogeneous production unit. The establishment lies half-way between in that it is an observable statistical unit but has a rather strong functional orientation.

It is important to note that the relationship between the two approaches is not symmetrical. The functional analysis depends on data generated in institutions. Transactions between these are what is observed in terms of economic value. Outside the transactions boundary this system does not apply.[2] Value as an observable variable is restricted to institutions that hold value as property and transact it between them. While production is certainly a necessary aspect of value, so is the institution. Only in a market economy that organises its division of labour on a monetary basis can the notion of value be rendered statistically observable. Outside such institutions it is speculative. The microeconomic theory of value ignores duality, implicitly postulating that institutional organisation and functional homogeneity coincide. In many cases this is true, in fact there are single establishment units. But it is the analytical distinction between the two that explains the concept of value as an observable quantity in economics. This brings us to one of the most controversial topics in national accounting (and in value theory): the definition of economic production.

Economic activity and the definition of production

The transactor/transaction principle: determination of the production boundary

An economy is defined as a national set of institutional units that contain production units, but there is no definition of what these units do. There must be activity (SNA, 1993, para. 4.2), but what is activity? The everyday meaning of this word is too broad and imprecise: the SNA must explain and define what it means by production.

This is a controversial, value-laden issue. Productivity has been a major ideology of institutions ever since medieval salvationist ideals ceded to modernist rationality. The production of services, as opposed to the production of goods, had to fight for theoretical and social recognition in the nineteenth century. Housework, subsistence production, and even production by nature became much debated issues in the twentieth century in this respect. The 1993 revision of the SNA was triggered by the perceived need to adjust GDP, find a 'true GDP' and so on. Yet despite the strong controversies it aroused, engaging many scholars outside the national accounting profession, the revised SNA retained essentially the same concept of production as the 1968 version. The modifications that were made were political rather than systemic in nature, and did not alter the theoretical content of the system.

As stated earlier, the definition of production is not a problem in microeconomic value theory, which assumes that this is evident. But it is a problem in economics and macroeconomic value theory. There are essentially three competing theories: one ties the concept of production to the transactor/transaction principle, the fundamental principle of national accounts; the second suggests that the concept of production should be based on the third-person principle; and the third, which is mostly found in economics textbooks, states that production is the satisfaction of wants, utility and scarcity. The 1993 SNA, being an inter-secretariat document by five political organisations and intended for practical use, does not, and need not, decide between these alternative dogmas. But in a theory of national accounts one ought to offer an opinion.

The methodological approach by which this opinion will be developed, matching theory with measurement, was introduced in Chapter 1, The national accounts claim to be a system. A system is different from a set of arbitrary conventions in that its conventions are logically related to one another. As a result one cannot change a rule or definition at only one point in the system. Systemic coherence requires that when considering a rule change the repercussions on all other entries, as well as on the system as a whole, be taken into account. In practice, of course, this logic may have to be modified. But such modifications must remain exceptions, required by specific circumstances, because if exceptional cases exceed regular cases in number and weight the conclusion must necessarily be drawn that the stated norm or concept of registration is not adequate for describing reality.

It has been customary to blame national accounting rules for the divergence of reality from economic theory. But the seemingly elementary option of adjusting statistical practice to value theory in its microeconomic form is fruitless. As the confirmation of standard practice in the 1993 SNA demonstrates, the statistical practice in measuring production cannot be changed. What may be, or rather should be, debated is its theoretical rationale. To provide a forum for such a debate is the purpose of the theory of national accounts. And in deciding between the different theories put forward, the most preferable is that which adheres to existing statistical practice most closely, minimising the need to find excuses for exceptions.

Let us demonstrate this by means of a famous historical example, namely the concept of market production. In the early national accounts manuals, and in many of today's textbooks, it is stated that national accounts are based on the production of goods or services for the market. Even the 1993 revision reiterated that the national accounts' 'main focus is the measure of output produced for the market and the income earned from that product' (Eisner, 1995, p. 91). If this is the rule then there is a need to explain why an enormous exception is made for government activity, which is typically non-market production.[3] If, on the other hand, paid employment, rather than production for sale, is chosen as the theoretical criterion of production, government activity is naturally included in GDP. Hence this, and not market production, appears to be an adequate theoretical concept to explain the practice of national accounting because it creates less exceptions. This suggestion is rarely found in the literature, but it is worth pursuing a little further.

In the Introduction the idea was put forward that there are two opposing theories when it comes to defining economic value. One derives its definition of production from the result (the good or service), the other defines production first and then looks for a product. Traditional microeconomic value theory chooses the first road, while practical necessities in terms of observation imply the second road for the national accounts. Proving the latter is not easy, because in the opinion of the writers of the SNA, micro-economic theory prevails and rules economic reasoning, including in respect of the national accounts, and one has taken some trouble to fit the SNA's reasoning to that precept. Under these circumstance the only possible way of arguing an alternative is to show the weaknesses in the reasoning of the microeconomic argument, to establish reasons for a different choice, and to prove that the weaknesses disappear when the direction of definition is reversed. We begin with the following proposition:

- Proposition 3.2: *production* is an activity by a person in an institutional unit, carried out regularly and against pay.

The first part of the definition will probably be found uncontroversial by the national accounting profession. The SNA itself stresses the institutional background of production: 'Economic production may be defined as an activity carried out under the control and responsibility of an institutional unit.... There must be an institutional unit that assumes responsibility for the process and owns any goods produced as outputs' (ibid., para. 6.15). This is an evocation of the institutional unit as the empirical unit of statistical observation. In order to obtain economic data there must first be an eco-nomic agent to produce them, and this agent will be the balance sheet holder. Without balance sheets or similar devices there can be no economic data and hence no national accounts.

With the second part of the definition, 'carried out regularly and against pay', we reach the pivotal point of our argument, and this may arouse controversy. But before we take a fresh look at the SNA production boundary and contemplate the standard arguments, let us recall our methodological approach. We take the practice of national accounting as given, and look for a concept of production that most closely resembles it. In the fourth revision of the SNA it was reaffirmed that the national accounts are based on the transactor/transaction principle. This is tantamount to saying that the data from which national accounts are constructed are transactions of value between transactors as owners of value (institutional units). These transac-tions are the statistical mass of events that are counted and collected in various economic surveys, then moulded into the system of national accounts. Whatever happens to them in terms of interpretation, or to use the technical term, of articulation, the bases of observations are these trans-actions. Now there is one particular transaction called 'compensation of employees'. The appearance of transactions of this kind in the accounts of an institutional unit is taken as proof in proposition 3.2 that the unit is economically active. If transactions are the data that generate national accounts, considering a particular transaction, namely the compensation of employees, as the indicator of economic activity is a natural way of analysing these data. And the result is not foreign to economic reasoning. Basing the definition of production on the transactor/transaction principle means that the production boundary of national accounts is essentially that of formal employment. In this way the traditional macro theory of employment and the theory of value are brought together in one descriptive system. This cannot be altogether wrong.

Employment takes two forms: dependent and independent. In the latter case the transaction that pays for the labour of the entrepreneur is the making of a withdrawal from his or her own account. This is questionable as a transaction because it occurs within one and the same institutional unit and we shall therefore treat it as a separate issue later in the text when we look at other boundary problems. For the moment we shall ignore the difference. It is uncontroversial that proposition 3.2 provides a sufficient condition of production in the accounts. In fact there is not a single exception. All paid labour is actually recognised as productive in the SNA. The controversial issue is whether proposition 3.2 is also a necessary condition of the production concept. This brings us to our next point.

The third-person principle

If we do not recognise the institutional nature of national accounts statistics we may choose to look for a purely physical definition of production. To do so it is necessary to modify one of our basic concepts. A transaction now becomes a broader event than just the creation of a claim–liability pair. 'A transaction consists of an inter-change, or inter-action, between two economic units which may take a variety of different forms' (Hill, 1977, p. 316). Such a vague definition cannot be used to draw a distinct boundary between production and other activities. The task is therefore to find another criterion to employ, and the third-person principle has come to be widely accepted for the purpose.

This principle distinguishes between goods and services. A good may be defined as a physical object that is appropriable and therefore transferable between economic units (ibid., p. 317). A service may be defined as a change in the circumstances of a person, or of a good belonging to some economic unit, as a result of the activity of some other economic unit, with the prior agreement of the person or the economic unit (ibid., p. 318). Or put more precisely: 'An economic service is one which may be done by someone other than the person benefiting therefrom' (Hawrylyshyn, 1977, p. 87).

In this theory the production of goods is always economic production, as is that of services if the third-person principle applies. The difficulty with the third-person principle is its vagueness. It says that a service is economic if it 'may' be done by someone other than the person who benefits from it. It does not define what a service is in the first place, nor who is the beneficiary.

And finally, the mere possibility of replacement by a third person calls for a very subjective assessment. Who decides what may be the case?

The third-person principle takes a functional point of view. It says that cleaning the house is economically the same irrespective of the institutional regime under which the cleaning is organised. Whether the work is paid for or not, the result is the same – a clean house. But this may be a superficial view in that it ignores important differences between clean houses. It is not self-evident that cleaning for someone else produces the same result as cleaning for oneself. In reality it is the other way round: the fact that certain work is paid for offers indisputable evidence that the work is done not for its own sake, but for someone else. Paid work testifies to the third-person concept, but it also implies that someone defines the output and result of the work, and is interested in minimising the input. This is the economic aspect. Thus paid labour signifies the existence of economic rationality, or at least in principle.

Unpaid work does not have to follow the norms of economic efficiency. Housewives and house husbands are their own bosses. To assign to their partner the role of a customer or a boss is beyond social reality. Division of labour in the household is governed by rules other than economic efficiency. In the same way as a car may be an investment or a consumer item depending on the institutional context in which it is used, rather than on whether the individual enjoys using it, so housework has different social and economic meanings that depend on whether it is carried out by a paid servant who has been trained in the routine of the work and is monitored for efficiency by the houshold head, or whether it is carried out by members of the household.

In order to show that the third-person principle cannot be generalised in the national accounts we shall look at the distinction between work and leisure. It goes without saying that valid answers to the question 'what do you do in your leisure time?' are 'play golf', 'go hunting' and 'walk the dog'. Even 'cleaning my room' can not be rejected if the person in question consciously classifies it this way. It is also clear that the same activities are work when they are made into a profession (golfer, hunter, housemaid). The third-person principle would then have to argue that the professional does work for his or her employer and can be replaced, while the hobbyist does it for him- or herself and therefore cannot be replaced. But this proves that the institutional context is decisive in deciding whether or not an activity falls within the production boundary.

Likewise eating, drinking, sleeping and learning are supposed to fall outside production under the third-person principle. But if an employee is sent on a higher education course at the expense of the employer, the latter must expect to profit from it or he or she would not pay. And the national accounts record it as an expense to the employer. If the same employer reimburses meal expenses, this is an indication of a third person profiting from another person's meal. And finally, if a person is paid for sleeping under certain experimental conditions, the payer has an interest in this person's sleep. One can say that in general the third-person principle has been applied selectively by researchers to certain activities that are unpaid and of benefit to someone else, but in order to use it consistently through the accounts one would have to identify as uneconomic all services that are paid for but are of no benefit to someone else. If there are none, this is proof that payment is accepted as the valid criterion to express benefit, and that there is no other objective criterion for the distinction in our economy.

The apparent popularity of the third-person principle is partly due to ambiguity. Activity can mean two things in the national accounts: it can stand for the data of an institution, or for the occupation of an individual. The third-person principle, finding ample application in time budgets and time-use studies, focuses on the individual. Institutional activity, however, is the organisation of abstract labour, blending different kinds of individual occupations indistinguishably into the overall functioning of the institution. It is an error of classification to confuse the activity of an institution with that of an individual.

As a last argument against the third-person principle we show that instead of defining production, the concept of output – or of goods and services – is dependent on the concept of production, having been defined prior to it. We would not know output from input if we did not have monetary transactions as an indicator of these flows. The SNA is quite explicit on this: 'Output is a concept that applies to a producer unit – an establishment or enterprise – rather than a process of production'. It consists of those goods and services that are produced within an establishment and become available outside it (SNA, 1993, para. 6.38) This is a clear indication of the institutional conditioning of the concepts of output and input. Without the property boundary of an institution, and the payment made in connection with it, the notions of output and input could not be defined.

That physical flows have nothing to do with value flows is clear from antipollution measures. Physical outflows are economic output if society reckons them as such, and this is signified by payments. When in the pollution abatement process the idea was born of turning at least some household and factory litter into valuable resources to be paid for, this litter became the basis of output instead of being ignored. Since institutional borders define what is output and what is input, it is from production as an institutional activity that we derive the concept of a good or a service as its result and not the other way round, as insinuated by the microeconomic approach. Hence we have:

- Proposition 3.3: *products* are production outputs delivered to individual units.

The utility or 'wants' principle

In the early days of the national accounts the concept of market production – realised, for example, in the United States and France (Studenski, 1958) – determined the production boundary, the rationale being that you sell your product and recuperate your outlays at the market so the market determines value. By the same token the market determines profit. With the adoption of the comprehensive production concept – to continue in Studenski's terminology – the present SNA production boundary was reached. Its rationale is the concept of formal employment, as shown above. Modifications of the boundary were called for in the process of revision, but apart from making minor adjustments the SNA stood firm. The comprehensive production boundary concept is accepted and institutionalised world-wide as the proper basis for compiling GDP.

The comprehensive production boundary is debatable between the economic theory of the national accounts and the standard theory of economics. Standard value theory has not fundamentally changed since the times of Marshall and Pigou. The national accounts have. They have switched from the market to the comprehensive production boundary as the area within which value is created, thus departing from the theory that the value of goods and services is determined only by the markets. The cleft is rarely recognised but it is there, and in its suppression it causes a lot of trouble to both professions. We suggest that modern theory should adapt itself, recognise the SNA's definition as adequate to describing the functioning of a modern economy, and incorporate it into its theory of production, income generation and value. To quote the SNA:

> The issues involved are not simply of a technical nature but raise fundamental questions of economic theory and principles. The concepts and classifications used in the System have a considerable impact on the ways in which the data may be used and the interpretations placed on them.
>
> (SNA, 1993, para. 1.19)

Quite independently of the national accounts, economic theorists have developed a standard set of propositions on production that are found in more or less the same form in all textbooks. We shall look at some of these, our choice being admittedly arbitrary but we hope not biased.

The 'theory of production', as it is explicitly called, is part of microeconomics. Not all textbooks bother to define production, and even when a definition is given it is not elaborated with care, but remains rather peripheral to the understanding of economics. Going by their subject index, Samuelson and Nordhaus (1989, p. 1006), for example, have a lot to say about 'conditions of production', 'theory of production', and above all 'the production function', but a definition of production as such is not offered.

In another book a typical statement is that production is 'any activity that creates present or future utility. Thus, for example the simple act of telling a joke constitutes production' (Frank, 1991, p. 253). This definition uses the term 'utility' as a definiens. The measurement of utility, either of individuals or of society as a whole, is beyond the range of statistical economic surveys. The example itself is obviously beyond the range of what can be measured as production in the national accounts.[4] Consequently the definition is not adequate for an economics concept based on the national accounts. A similar argument applies when the definition is made somewhat more explicit: 'Goods and services are the means by which people seek to satisfy some of their wants. The act of making goods or services is called production' (Lipsey and Steiner, 1981, p. 6). Although goods and services expressly appear in this definition, the latter ultimately depends on the definition and thus measurement of wants. We take it that wants are synonymous with utility in this context.

A more accounting-like definition is provided by the following: 'Production may be equivalently described as a process that transforms inputs (factors of production) into outputs' (Frank, 1991, p. 254). This definition is equivalent to the one for goods and services, according to the author, because 'output is something that creates present or future utility' (ibid., p. 254). The definition entails something like an accounting structure, with inputs on one side of the account and outputs on the other. But apart from this formal analogy, the concept of output as something that 'creates' utility not only blurs the concept of production (how can output, which has been created, itself create utility – is this a second form of production?) but is also outside the realm of measurement.

Salvatore (1994, p. A-52) defines production as 'the transformation of resources of inputs into outputs of goods and services'. This calls for an explanation of goods and services. According to Salvatore a good is 'a commodity of which more is preferred to less' (ibid., p. A-47), but the author fails to tell us what a commodity is. To show how inoperative the definition is, let us play with it. What happens if more of a good is preferred by a person when she or he is hungry and less after she or he has eaten? The definition does not address the question of storing value in time.

In the words of McConnell (1984, p. 17), 'Let us emphatically add that the overall end or objective of all economic activity is the attempt to satisfy these diverse material wants'. Although microeconomics sometimes assumes this emphatic thrust of claiming uniqueness over all economics, few authors are aware that this requires them to justify and explain the national accounts production concept. A quite sophisticated definition reads: 'In the economic sense production means the transformation of a commodity into something which is regarded as "different" by some consumers, although it may be physically unchanged.' (Lancaster, 1973, p. 28). What if it is regarded as different by some but not by others? How is a statistician to know about these consumer perceptions? This is where national accountants, and price statisticians express disappointment with a theory that abounds with sparkling examples ('telling a joke') but ignores the requirements of measurement and observation. Naturally this is mirrored in shoulder shrugging by economists about the inability of statistics to meet the requirements of theory. The concept and method split is felt on both sides of the economics river but is not properly addressed by either.[5]

Actually the diversion of concepts has repercussions even within the theoretical mainstream. It is known as the unsolved aggregation problem from microeconomic theory to macroeconomics. Let us therefore look at macroeconomic definitions of production, which is the field to which the national accounts apply directly. Again we find a general leniency in the handling of the issue. For example 'gross domestic product (GDP) is the total value of the current production of final goods and services within the national territory during a given period of time, normally a quarter or a year' (Sachs and Larrain, 1993, p. 16). In spite of its apparent precision the most important definition is missing, namely that of production. Sometimes even this definition is mistreated: real national product is 'the total market value of all goods and services produced in an economy during a year' (Lipsey and Steiner, 1981, p. 491). It is neither market value – given the extensive share of non-market production – nor all goods and services, as the greater portion is produced for intermediate use and is not counted in GDP. Even a Nobel laureate is not immune to this mistake: 'What is gross national product? It is the name we give to the total dollar value of the goods and services produced by a nation during a given year.' (Samuelson and Nordhaus, 1989, p. A-52; see also Lancaster, 1973, p. 377).

One can even find logical full-circles: production is 'the man-made process of generating products.' and products are 'the result of the production and goals of an enterprise' (*Gablers Wirtschaftslexikon*, 1988, p. 1006). The second part of the latter quote does not actually provide a definition, but put together the two quotes suggest that production is the generation of products, and products are generated by production.

If general macroeconomic textbooks offer little on the concept of production, books on national accounts proper can not get away so easily. 'The comprehensive production concept is broader than the market-oriented concept and the material production concept. It basically considers the creation of all goods and services irrespective of whether or not they touch the market' (Brümmerhoff, 1995, p. 63). In this definition we see a mixture of theory and practice. Market independence is recognised, production is defined by means of goods and services, but the latter are not defined. This step is taken by Chapron and Séruzier (1984, p. 20): 'By means of a classification the national accounts define the list of all goods and services that are disposable in a country.' The classification defines these goods and services, but what defines the scope of the classification?

Some national accounts authors have not even perceived the market independence of the SNA production concept. 'As before, production is defined largely in terms of goods and services produced for and traded in markets.' (Kendrick, 1995, p.12): the NIPA and the SNA 'share the essential property of being market oriented.' (Eisner, 1995, p. 91). To say that 'the SNA starts from a market-oriented production boundary... [and] some well-defined, non-market output by "recognised producers" are included in production' (Holub, 1994, p. 285), is more precise, but conveys the impression that the rules for national accounts are made up in an *ad hoc* rather than a systematic way. Also the statement 'The concept of national product is essentially oriented towards market outputs. Hence non-market outputs remain outside the national product' (Frenkel and John, 1991, p.144) is too crude for even new students to find acceptable.

The literature conveys the idea to users of national accounts that inclusion of non-market production is an exception to the pure concept of the national accounts' production boundary, this pure concept being market production. This idea may have been true in the beginning. Now, although it has gone largely unnoticed, one of the important results of the fourth revision of the SNA is that the *Economica* controversy involving Kuznets and Hicks has been decided, once and for all. The fact that non-market production is part of GDP is not given a single explanatory sentence in the 1993 SNA. This fact must be theoretically appreciated when defining the pure production boundary concept. Actually, microeconomic theory as such does not support the market restriction as it deals with wants and scarcity that may well exist outside the market. Microeconomic theory replaces the notion of institutional activity, as employed in the national accounts, with the concept of scarcity of goods as its measure of value, and this may well exist outside the market. So the question remains of where the reason for the persistence of the misconception might lie. Apart from mere tradition there may be a practical reason. The definition of output and input is easier for market sectors, which live on sales, than for non-market sectors that depend on other revenues. The input–output framework is more naturally applied to market than to non-market sectors, and this structural feature may support the bias in concept.

There is one area in which the market orientation of national accounts can be defended as essential. If one wishes to pass from nominal to real value accounting for the value change of the general unit of value – money – the market of products becomes the crucial field of observation. This will be dealt with extensively in Chapter 5.

The compromise of the SNA

Our contention is that in the theory of national accounts the national production boundary is defined by proposition 3.2 and is probably met with resistance by national accountants themselves. In order to support it we claim that this definition has the advantage of minimising discrepancies between theory and practice. Put the other way around, this is the definition that best explains standard practice. We take the 1993 SNA as a useful summary of that practice, and show that its deviations from the above definition of the production boundary are either insignificant or can be explained as exceptions that have been made for certain extra purposes other than the main purpose of measuring production. The SNA, having been established by coordination of several independent political bodies (United Nations, OECD etc.), must necessarily find a compromise between differing theoretical views. Still in essence it conforms to proposition 3.2 as we now show.

It has already been explained that the inclusion of non-market production should not be seen as an exception but as fully in accordance with proposition 3.2. In fact it represents one of its supporting arguments under the premise of uniting theory with measurement. The major exception of the SNA production boundary to proposition 3.2 is the production imputed to occupiers of their own houses. During public discussions on the fourth revision of the SNA this exception was not questioned. Given the general pressure for increased imputations, no need was felt to expel, or at least to rationalise, an old imputation. Income from owner-occupied housing is a historical relict of the time, when national accounts were built and took their first conventions from neighbouring fields. In order to put owners and renters of homes on equal footing, tax authorities imputed an additional income to owners of their own shelter as property. The other possible option – making the rent on shelter tax deductible – might have been admissible on equity grounds, and would have been more in line with the transaction principle, but apparently it was not considered. In any case the inclusion is a device to present some kind of welfare measurement in the national accounts. The related activities and economic behaviour are quite different in the two cases: The attitudes and experiences of people who live in rented houses are not comparable to those of people who live in their own houses. Owners are not economically rational in respect of their living quarters. There is perhaps a tendency towards overinvestment, that is to apply more expenditure and capital than professional management would deem necessary. Since profit is not measured or even thought about, nothing is known about such data or ratios, and valuation is a mere analogy.

The inclusion of goods produced for own use is rationalised in the SNA because at the time of production one rarely knows how much is destined for the market and how much will be retained for own use (SNA, 1993, para. 6.23) This is a practicality criterion, and it relies on insignificance as far as the amounts are concerned. The 1993 SNA also includes subsistence production, that is, production where the major share of the goods produced is not destined for the market. (We take up this exception to the transaction principle in the following section.)

The SNA summarises activities that fall within the production boundary as follows (ibid., para. 6.18):

a) The production of goods or services supplied to other units than their producers.
b) The production of all goods on own account.
c) The own account services of owner-occupiers.

Considering that production is by definition an activity by institutional units that pay their employees through wages and their entrepreneurs through withdrawals from own account, this definition more or less coincides with the transaction definition given in proposition 3.2.

The proof of the pudding is in the eating. If we put forward the concept of formal activity as the characteristic feature of the SNA production boundary we must show that this concept explains standard practice better than any other concept in that it minimises the amount of required exceptions.

Before we do so a word is in order about the role of exceptions in empirical work. As already stated, when constructing a pure concept one abstracts from certain features of reality. So it is natural when applying a pure concept that there will be exceptions, which may be of different origin. One is the realisation of a second purpose. The multipurpose dimension of the national accounts is well known and the subject of much controversy. Another origin of exceptions is technical. A concept usually cannot be applied without some adaptation of the measurement apparatus, although the nature of this apparatus should be reflected in the concept. A third important reason is historical continuity. National accounting concepts may have acquired a meaning beyond mere theory during their historical passage. This calls for the retention of rules that under a purely theoretical, and newly clarified, concept appear as impurities. But whatever the reason for the exception, one rule is applied with rigour in all cases: an exception must not destroy its concept. It must be quantitatively insignificant if it is rightly to be called an exception. Otherwise it will consume the concept and become the concept itself.

The inclusion of non-market production as a natural part of GDP has destroyed the old market concept inasmuch as this addresses the markets for goods and services. On the other hand it has stopped not at an arbitrary boundary, but at one that is equally well defined by transactions, the market of factors, and of labour in particular. We will show how the concrete recommendations of the SNA can be defended if this shift in conceptual focus is accepted. Table 3.2 summarises the individual items and the arguments in the SNA about the production boundary. The reader is urged to refer to the original SNA document for the details, because many of the fine points made in the original are ignored here for reasons of space.

Table 3.2   Summary of the SNA production boundary concept

Production item	Relationship to SNA boundary	Claimed rationale
Individual or collective goods or services supplied to users other than their producers	Included	Definition of SNA concept
Own account production of domestic and personal services	Excluded	Self-contained activity within households
Domestic and personal services by paid domestic staff	Included	None given
Own-account production of goods	Included	Indistinguishability of user
Own-account production of housing services	Included	International and inter-temporal comparisons
Do-it-yourself decoration, maintenance and small repairs	Excluded	Subgroup of domestic services
Illegal production	Included	Coherence of accounts
Concealed production	Included	Productive in an economic sense

Source: SNA (1993), paras 6.17–36.

Individual or collective goods or services supplied to units other than those which produce them fall inside the boundary, by definition. The applied rationale is that of third-unit, that is, the consuming unit must be different from the producing one, which is one way of expressing the transactor/ transaction principle. This criterion is part of the definition of an economic good or service in the SNA. But the definition is also meant to include non-market production inasmuch as it is formally conducted for others. The wording of the SNA still clings extensively to the goods and services market, but we have shown this to be conceptually inadequate and unnecessary. We may say, therefore, that this item in Table 3.2 is the core of production considered in the SNA. It represents the typical case, and falls clearly within the production boundary. All other items lie on the boundary, that is, they may be debated.

Own-account production is generally excluded from the production boundary as a logical consequence of the transaction principle. This was debated in the course of the SNA revision because 'a considerable amount of labour is devoted to the production of these domestic and personal services while their consumption makes an important contribution to economic welfare' (ibid., para. 6.21). However the fact that these services are not part of a market exchange process implies that:

- They have limited repercussions on the rest of the economy.
- There are typically no suitable market prices that can be used to value such services.
- Imputed values are not equivalent to monetary values for analytical or policy purposes (ibid., para. 6.21).

In short the exclusion of these services is a matter of being consistent with the transactions definition of national accounts.[6]

To give this exclusion more theoretical substance, let us remember that the criterion of whether or not labour is paid is not an accidental one. Payment for labour (that is, the value transaction) and the associated formal requirements are expressions of labour's social organisation and incorporation into the overall division of labour ruling the economy and reflected in the system. Paid labour is subjected to direction by the owners of capital, who define its efficiency. Unpaid labour can be performed under quite different regimes of effort and satisfaction. By the same token, paid domestic or personal services lie within the boundary (Table 3.2, item 3).[7]

The convention of including the production of all goods irrespective of whether they are for third units or own use is based on an interesting argument: 'At the time the production takes place it may not even be known whether, or in what proportions, the goods produced are destined for the market or for own use' (ibid., para. 6.24). It follows that when this is known the appropriate judgement can be made. A chemical substance, for example, that is produced in a factory and fully consumed in another production activity in that factory is not a good by definition, even if it is marketed by other factories. A borderline case is when part of the product is sold and part is consumed. This is a technical rather than a conceptual question, and in order to clarify the boundary the SNA recommends the inclusion of all primary products from agriculture, mining, water supply or other activities that are typical of developing countries. We have an exception on technical grounds.

Own-account housing services are an exception to the rule of third-unit consumption, as the SNA itself observes. The reason for making this exception is that 'the ratio of owner-occupied to rented dwellings can vary significantly between countries and in even over short periods of time within a single country, so that both international and intertemporal comparisons . . . could be distorted if no imputation were made' (ibid., para. 6.29). Whatever the underlying rationale, calling it an exception corroborates the rule and the underlying boundary concept. Living in one's own house is not a formal activity, of course, so this recommendation is an exception not under the goods and services concept, based on utility, but under the activity concept, based on transactions (or the product market concept for that matter). If the SNA calls it an exception it reinforces the second of these concepts. The exclusion of do-it-yourself decoration and repairs is justified by the general rule of excluding all internal household services, as explained above. While it is hard to justify under the third-person principle, the concept of formal employment or activity explains the exclusion naturally. Do-it-yourself is by its very nature an activity that is performed outside the formal organisation of the division of labour.

The inclusion of illegal and concealed production (the last items in Table 3.2) raises the problem of where to draw the boundary between formal and informal activity. We reserve this discussion for the next section. Transactions are defined as the creation of credit and liability between units that can be sued. Clearly illegal transactions are performed without such a safeguard. An important element of formality is thus missing. A similar argument holds for hidden production, which may occur outside the transactions boundary for various reasons of concealment.

Summarising our proof, we find that item 1 (non-market production) is directly explained by the formal activity criterion and is an exception under the product market criterion. Items 2 and 3 (domestic and personal services) are directly explained by the concept of formal employment, but they are difficult to explain under the product market concept because the product is not really marketed (own account production), while if it is paid the activity is marketed. Own-account production of goods (item 4) is an exception under the activity concept on technical grounds, as it is under the product market concept. It would not be an exception under the utility concept, but the latter is not utilised in statistics. Do-it-yourself activities lie outside the boundary under both concepts of production – product market and activity market – while illegal and concealed production are borderline cases in both concepts.

At the boundary of economic production: quasi-corporations, self-employment and informal activity

The sequence of institutions within the national accounts

So far in this chapter we have concentrated on establishing the transactor/ transaction principle as the theoretical borderline of economic activity in the national accounts. But no theory can explain all cases that occcur in reality because reality is more diverse than the abstraction of a theory allows for. Thus every theory has its borderline cases and boundary problems. These are cases that resist classification in that they do not fit well into either of the defined categories. Borderline cases give rise to exceptions to a theoretical rule, which are inevitable as a concession to reality. However they should be of minor weight if the theory is to stand. Exceptions that exceed the rule in terms of quantitative importance are not borderline cases but cases against the attempted theory. In this section we take up such borderline cases, discussing them on the basis of the transactor/transaction principle. This will be an opportunity to probe into and corroborate proposition 3.2.

Recognising a boundary implies that one keeps a certain distance from the object under investigation. It is a common experience in empirical observation that the closer one approaches a boundary the less one can distinguish it from its surrounding environment. Boundaries are drawn, not discovered. Maintaining distance allows one to keep in mind the whole set of objects under study and their common features, as opposed to all other objects. Hence in order clearly to identify the institutional character of the SNA production boundary these institutions must be studied. We have already dealt with the overall definition (see the section on institutional units above). More insight can be gained by detailing the classification of institutional units and exposing their essential characteristics. The SNA devotes quite some effort and intellectual analysis to the issue. We shall attempt to summarise the text without losing its essential message.

The main criteria by which institutional units are classified are:

- Market versus non-market.
- Profit versus non-profit.
- Incorporated versus unincorporated.

Also to be remembered is the dissimilarity between institutional units and households in terms of defining criteria, as mentioned earlier (see Figure 3.1). We will study the application of these criteria to different types of unit in order to gain a clear vision of the boundary of institutional production (that is, formal production), which will allow us to transgress that boundary and make valid inferences about what may then be called informal production.

The ideal institution in the SNA's terms is the non-financial corporation. It owns property and accounts for it on a balance sheet, hence it creates economic data. It produces for the market, hence it has sales that are transformed into value added. And it pays wages, and thus measures its input of labour. However the so-called 'non-financial corporations sector' includes other types of organisations: quasi-corporations and certain non-profit institutions. The first boundary issue, then, involves the differences between these organisations and the corporation, and why in spite of these differences they are included in the non-financial corporative sector.

Quasi-corporations are unincorporated enterprises that are operated as though they are corporations. The main difference between them and actual corporations is that they have no legal identity apart from that of their owners. Thus they do not own property or accept liabilities in their own right. But they produce for the market, pay wages and take credit, which means they operate like corporations. If they function like corporations they must keep a complete set of accounts, and this is a necessary condition for being recognised as a quasi-corporation (SNA, 1993, para. 4.51). In other words an organisation that does not keep a complete set of accounts cannot be treated as a quasi-corporation. For this reason it is often said that the institutional unit in the national accounts is the smallest unit to keep a complete set of accounts. This is a natural definition, because it is from these accounts that one generates the economic data required for the national accounts.

Like corporations, non-profit institutions have a legal identity of their own, but they differ in that their profits must not be distributed to their owners (ibid., para. 4.54). They are classified into market and non-market producers according to their way of gaining revenue, and are found in the corporate, governmental, and household sectors. They compile balance sheets, of course, if only for the purpose of declaring their financial management to the tax authorities. Included in the non-financial corporative sector are private, non-profit institutions that serve businesses: because of this they are also defined as market producers (ibid., para. 4.59).

Hence the theoretical definition given earlier of an institutional unit as a legal entity in its own right is enlarged to include all units that keep a set of accounts (quasi-corporations) for practical purposes. This makes sense, because it is accounts and not legal rights that directly generate economic data. A unit may be market or non-market oriented, profit or non-profit oriented, incorporated or unincorporated, but if it maintains a complete set of accounts it is an institutional unit and thus lies within the production boundary. Remember, though, that fulfilment of a property criterion, such as holding a set of accounts, is not sufficient for a unit to be designated as a productive unit and some activity must be carried out by that unit. The payment of wages is sufficient as an indicator of employment. This brings us to the question of self-employment, which is a typical boundary problem. Self-employment is found neither in the corporate nor in the government sector. Consequently we can say that for these two sectors proposition 3.2 holds as a description of the production boundary of the SNA, as these are the major sectors in an economy. Thus our boundary problem has narrowed down to the household sector.

Households are not institutional units. In a way they represent a reversal of the hierarchy of defining criteria. While institutional units are defined as holders of one property that contains one or more establishments, households are defined as living quarters (which is equivalent to an establishment) that contain at least one person who is a natural property holder. Households may or may not be productive. Households may own unincorporated enterprises, or more precisely, certain members of a household may be the holders of such property. If these enterprises maintain a balance sheet and a complete set of accounts, they are grouped into the corporate sector; if not, they are grouped into the household sector as an 'integral part' of households (ibid., para. 4.151). Such enterprises can range from single persons working as street traders or shoe cleaners through to large manufacturing, construction or service enterprises with many employees (ibid., para. 4.144). It is hard to see how the latter could be managed without a balance sheet, if only for tax purposes. Such cases are probably an exception. In general, unincorporated household enterprises consist of self-employed owners with a few employees. As long as these employees are paid the enterprise meets proposition 3.2 and falls within the theoretical production boundary. This leaves single entrepreneurs, and possibly their family members, as the only borderline case to decide.

Self-employed workers are persons who own the enterprise in which they work. The enterprise is neither a separate legal entity nor a separate institutional unit. Consequently self-employed persons receive a 'mixed income' as owners of and workers at their enterprise. 'Entrepreneurial income' was the earlier and somewhat more concrete definition of this type of income. The theoretical question is whether receipt of such income can be considered a transaction, because only if it is can we subsume the corresponding production under the transactor/transaction principle.

According to the SNA (para, 17.7) 'A job is like transaction', meaning that a job is an institutional shell that is filled by the activity of employees. Does a self-employed worker have a job? If the enterprise is a market enterprise the answer is positive because the selling of products gives rise to transactions at economically significant prices, and probably at a scale that requires regular purchases of inputs as well. Even if no accounts are kept a certain distinction between intermediate and final use of such purchases will operate, so that a value added statement can be compiled. Unincorporated, profit-oriented market enterprises fall within the transactor/transactions boundary of production (Figure 3.2).

This leaves non-market household enterprises to be decided upon. In the SNA these are viewed as producing for their own final use, which is consumption. There are practically no sales, the distinction between intermediate and final use is loose, especially as an enterprise normally has no final consumption, and values and efficiency are only marginally controlled in the daily life of this organisation. These activities lie outside the transactions boundary.

The SNA includes the production of all goods by households in GDP, as well as two kinds of service: owner-occupied housing and domestic servants. We have dealt with these issues above, explaining that they are exceptions to the transactions principle, and why they are included despite this. Without these exceptions the production boundary defined by proposition 3.2 would run neatly between household unincorporated market enterprises and enterprises producing for own use. Furthermore, if the formal boundary is theoretically sound in that it corresponds to the fundamental traits of social and economic organisation in global society it can help us to understand a complementary concept: the informal economy, to which we now turn.

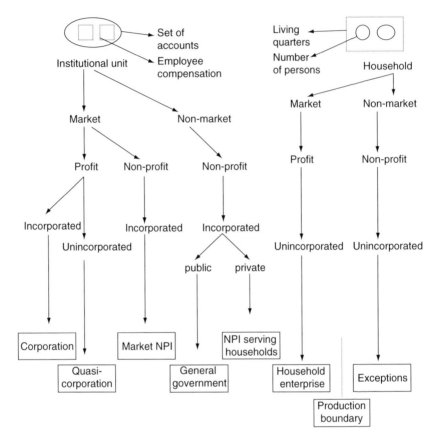

Figure 3.2 The characteristics of units within the SNA production boundary

The concept of informal production

At the start of the fourth revision of the SNA the deficiencies of the 1968 SNA were discussed and the lack of concern for typical issues in developing countries was generally acknowledged. Uma Choudhury (1986), examining the revision programme from the point of view of developing countries, pointed out that understanding and implementing the SNA in its totality would not be easy and would involve problems of interpretation and measurement, and that 'the production boundary, the coverage of the household sector, the definition of the informal sector and the measurement of its activity are all important questions to be resolved if the estimates of national income in these countries are to be realistic' (ibid., p.122).

The 1993 SNA responded to this challenge, basically by extending its production boundary. The general message seems to be that as much informal activity as possible should be included, but relatively little attention was paid to problems of measurement, or to discussing the adequacy of the system for representing this area of production. In fact, instead of presenting new text on the subject, two pages from an ILO document on the informal sector were reproduced as an annex to Chapter IV. As this was the only instance where the SNA relied on an import, this may be interpreted as a sign of unease and uncertainty about moving into this field.

The question of informal production is not confined to the developing world – although it is prevalent there, increasing unemployment has led to informal activity in developed countries as well. The boundary between formal and informal production is important in all countries of the world, and must be defined within a theoretical concept, notwithstanding the technical difficulties of its realisation. We deal with the issue in two steps. First we try to establish a concept of informal production by looking at the phenomena studied by social scientists and experts in the field. Then we look briefly at how this concept might be incorporated into the national accounts.

Starting with a terminological remark, it has become customary to speak of the informal 'sector', a word that has been adopted by social scientists as a general expression without regard to its use in the national accounts. Within the framework of the national accounts the term 'sector' is strictly defined as a class of institutional units. Informal units are just the opposite of such institutions. Thus we cannot properly speak of the 'informal sector' of the economy. It is preferable to use expressions such as 'informal activity' or 'informal production' in order to avoid confusion.

Informal production is first of all a very heterogeneous phenomenon. Defined as it is in opposition to formal production it contains all manner of activities that among themselves are not homogeneous. Following Teichert (1993) we distinguish five broad areas where people are economically active (Figure 3.3). The first is the formal economy, organised into agriculture, manufacturing, services, public administration and so on. Then there is the shadow economy, which includes moonlighting, tax fraud and illegal and concealed activities. The third area is the subsistence economy, which includes do-it-yourself activities and probably should include subsistence agriculture. The fourth area is housework, or the household economy more generally. The final area consists of self-help organisations, including volunteer work, neighbourhood help and perhaps also extended family help. Teichert's analysis is restricted to Germany, but his categories are applicable to other societies as well.

The shadow economy is almost as formal as the visible economy. It may conceal itself from the eye of the government, but it is part and parcel of the economic capital circuit. Proof of this is the fact that in most cases it fulfils the criteria of market production, which puts it into the enterprise sector. This is the 'unregistered' part of the formal economy (Mulder, 1996), and to include it in the system is in line with the concept of formal activity analysed above, under the technical purpose of comprehensiveness, or 'exhaustiveness' as it is now called (Calzaroni *et al.*, 1996). Enterprises in the shadow economy conceal some or all of their transactions from the government, but they function in all markets (products, labour, capital) in an ordinary way. There is a certain theoretical flaw in respect of the institutional formality of such enterprises in that they cannot really 'sue and be sued' for their transactions, but this is more a formal flaw than one of substance.

Not all unregistered activity is formal, of course. The three areas on the right-hand side of Figure 3.3 represent the informal part of the economy. They have in common the fact that their activities are not performed within enterprises or the public sector, the typical formal sectors. The SNA excludes the first two kinds of activity (self-help and household activities), but places the third (subsistence activity) within its production boundary. What is the rationale for this? It is clear that both the self-help economy and the household economy exist outside the transactions boundary, and for this reason are rightly excluded. So why is the subsistence economy, which is also mainly own-use production, included? Subsistence production exists in rural areas where people engage in traditional farming and have little market access. It also exists in towns, although the activities are different. The urban branch of the subsistence economy is what is called the informal sector in the SNA. It is 'a circuit of parallel production', which has 'its foundation in the inadequacy of the regulatory role of government and in the general economic crisis that has raged for two decades' (Rashidi, 1996, p.18).

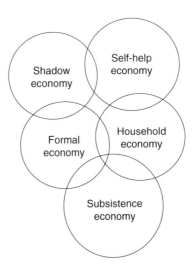

Figure 3.3   Classification of individual activities carried out in society

The existence of an unregulated, informal urban economy was officially recognised in the early 1970s following the observation in several developing countries that a massive number of new entrants to the labour force were failing to show up in the formal employment statistics (Todaro, 1989). They were found to be earning a living from activities that ranged from hawking, street vending, letter writing, knife sharpening and junk collecting to selling fireworks, drug peddling, prostitution and snake charming. Subsequent studies revealed that 20 per cent of the labour force in Colombo and 70 per cent in the urban areas of Pakistan were working informally. Most of the workers who enter this economy are recent migrants from rural areas who are unable to find employment in the formal economy. Their aim is usually to obtain enough income to survive rather than to make a profit. Most inhabit shacks in slums or squatter settlements – 'informal' housing, as it is called academically which lack public services – but many are homeless, living on pavements or in parks.

Oladoye (1996), in line with the ILO document mentioned above,[8] lists the characteristic features of such activities:

- The enterprises are family owned.
- They operate in unregulated markets.
- They are small in terms of scale of operation and capital.
- They have no external sources of finance or materials.
- They employ skills acquired outside the formal school system.
- There are no fixed working hours or days.

By inversion, this list also defines the criteria of formal activity, namely that the institution that owns the property is separated from individuals, that the markets are regulated by law, that the scale of operation is possibly very large, that external finance and materials are supplied, and that labour is formally trained and formally employed. All this may be condensed into the phrase 'formal activity is production organised through capital', so informal production is production without capital, or non-capitalist production, with all the difference in values and behaviour that this entails and cannot logically be part of the formal economy. The two areas are distinct.

Searching for a line of demarcation

When defining the boundary between formal and informal production one must be aware of two levels of operation: the conceptual level and the technical level. The first is where we work with theory, logic and axioms, the second has to take account of feasibility and practical conventions. This is our concern in this section.

Let us first summarise our findings on the formal production boundary. In the national accounts this boundary is based on the transaction principle of paid labour and the concept of activity by an institution. The presence of both is a necessary condition for measuring production, with money as the means of comparison and the store of value. Typical of this activity is a high degree of formalisation in respect of labour organisation, official regulation and the financing and control of capital, to which the system with its various accounts adequately corresponds. The formal 'system' is the accounting mirror image of the formal economy.

Logically speaking an economy that is not governed by formal institutions and property transactions cannot be subject to observation through the national accounts because it does not generate the data required to make the system work. In dwelling on the household sector the SNA conveys the impression that – in its desire to be comprehensive – it would like to include all informal activities, but in our view this intention is contrary to its own perception as a system. Not only do the accounts of the system have nothing to do with the economics of such ventures, but also the impossibility of gathering the necessary data should be sufficient proof of its non-applicability. It does not make sense to provide such analytical tools as an input–output table for an economy that does not use outside resources, or to impute a GDP on the production account, and then to carry this number untouched through all the distribution and expenditure accounts where none of these functions actually occur. Although technically elegant, such a procedure provides no explanatory information on the estimated variable, and it distorts the accounts.

One might argue pragmatically that a concept is never applied in purity, and that as the national accounts already allow for some exceptions to the transaction principle, these should be extended to make GDP more meaningful. However this argument is potentially self-destructive. The methodology of working with concepts and classifications requires that definitions are not modified during the measurement process. If for the national accounts we postulate the principles of a formal economy, but in practice refute them by having the major part of production taking place outside the formal economy, there can be no coherent meaning at all. Exceptions are necessary to adapt a concept to practical observations. But if they are overwhelming in number they disrupt the concept, and should be theoretically recognised as doing so.

The SNA includes the production of goods, irrespective of the institutional circumstances in which it occurs, and excludes services when they occur outside the transactions boundary. This is a workable convention (taken over from the European system) and it has a certain rationale as goods can be counted physically. We will not probe into the theoretical grounds or practical feasibility of this convention, but in the European countries from which it stems its significance is small enough to call it an exception. For other countries the weights are distributed quite differently. Picking an arbitrary example (Rashidi, 1996), in Zaire for the year 1992 a value of 2437 billion zaires was imputed to the subsistence economy, mainly agriculture, and

Table 3.3   Economic activity in Zaire, 1992 (billion zaire)

Sector	Formal	Informal	Traditional	Total activity
Agriculture	192	–	2404	2596
Extraction of minerals	171	72	–	243
Foods, drinks, tobacco	49	39	–	88
Other manufacturing	108	65	–	173
Water and electricity	229	–	–	229
BTP	41	59	33	133
Wholesale and retail trade	134	1081	–	1251
Transport and telecommunications	144	61	–	205
Market services	114	337	–	451
Non-market services	120	–	–	120
All sectors	1302	1741	2437	5453

1714 billion zaires was estimated for the urban informal economy, mainly retail trade, compared with a formal GDP of only 1302 billion zaire (or 24 per cent of the reported total production) from institutional units proper in the SNA sense (Table 3.3). To include such lump sums in GDP changes the very meaning of this term.

Rigid distinction between formal and informal activities is called for at the conceptual level, in the sense that national accounts are designed to describe a perfect, fully institutionalised capitalist economy. They are not valid for all productive activities that exist in a dual or otherwise segregated economy. It is conceivable that if more and more regulations were to erode, if smuggling, bribery and so on were to grow, in short, if informality came to characterize more and more institutions of an economy, this would result directly in a lower adequacy of national accounts as a controlling device for such an economy. In reality the boundary between formal and informal activities is fuzzy and must be defined and redefined with history. This is indicated in Figure 3.3 by the overlapping circles of activities. It may not always be clear where a certain activity belongs, and some may belong to more than one category. Precision in operating the theoretically defined production boundary is achieved through experience and continued statistical efforts.

For such efforts two roads are open. The first is that compilation of a value for informal activities is not forbidden, of course. If it is placed outside the core accounts in a standard table – or more elaborately, in a satellite account – it conveys useful information about orders of magnitude without insinuating a false circuit of value through the economy. In fact registration as a distinctive kind of 'GDP', as in Table 3.3, seems to be the natural statistical reaction to the problem of incomparability. Money functions here only as an accounting unit, not as a means of exchange or a store of value. It is itself used as an informal measure.[9] The second road starts with recognition of the fact that a boundary can be drawn more precisely if it is approached from both sides. This calls for an accounting system that includes activities other than those performed by institutions, namely those carried out by individuals during their 24-hour day. The natural unit for measuring such personal activity is time (Goldschmidt-Clermont and Pagnossin-Aligisakis, 1996). Consequently it seems that a secure and well-defined boundary between the formal activity of institutions and the individual activity of persons in such institutions, as well as their informal activity outside, can be found by building a bridge between national accounts of economic value and an accounting system for the use and appropriation of time.

This completes our exposition of the basic structure of national accounts in nominal terms. We have spelled out four propositions that have paved the systematic way from value transactions as observable data to product values as the purpose of analysis via institutional and production units as the creators of these data and generators of products. These propositions were elaborated in detail because the definition of production is not only important in itself but is also pivotal to the definitions that follow. Thus the complement to production – consumption – follows immediately.

- Proposition 3.4: *consumption* is the use of products that are not destined for production.

In order to be more precise, one might use proposition 3.4 to define final consumption rather than intermediate consumption. As an example of the dependence of the consumption concept on the definition of production, take the exception to the transactor/transaction principle of owner-occupied housing. Speaking in terms of transactions, people living in their own houses buy consumer goods when they buy material, for renovation or repair. Under the rule that living in a house is counted as production, such purchases take on the character of production inputs and are registered as intermediate goods. In this way the definition of production also determines what is (final) consumption.

Part II
Real Accounts

4
The Index Number Problem

The purpose of national accounts is to compare economic parameters in time and space. However nominal values, which are the value of transactions between institutions, are not directly comparable in this way. They must be controlled for changes in the purchasing power of the transaction unit: money. This chapter investigates the procedures employed in this process, focusing on the recommendations of the SNA, namely the Geary–Khamis index and the chained Fisher index for comparisons in space and time. A theory of relativity of value is inferred, resulting from the necessity of working with commodity bundles as the standard of value in spatial and temporal comparisons. A scheme for integrating these two dimensions in one coherent system is proposed.

Methodological introduction: the charms of realness

The standard presentation of money value in textbooks and journals

It has been emphasised more than once in this book that the existence of a general means of payment is crucial for the measurement and concept of value, but the question has been left open of how to measure the value of this means of payment. This is the problem of accounting in 'real' terms and ought now to be investigated. It will take about the same effort as before to expose its main principles, which have emerged less from national accounts departments than from the longer tradition of price statistics. In any event they are of the same importance in respect of value theory as the principles applied to the purely nominal accounts.

   The figures in national accounts are stated in some or other monetary unit, for example dollars or pounds. These units, which express economic value, have three functions: they express value as a means of payment, they serve as a unit of accounting and they act as a store of value, the three forms being mutually interdependent. If money is thus the measuring rod of value, the question arises of the quality of this measurement device. We know from everyday experience that the measuring rod is not constant over time or in space. Over time there is high or low inflation, sometimes also deflation. In space there are different currencies, the mutual value of which is regulated on international markets. In the absence of a strong national central bank, different currencies might even circulate within one country, their value being matched against each other.

The value of a currency is determined by means of certain statistical indices, such as the Geary–Khamis index for comparisons in space and the chained Fisher index for comparisons over time, as recommended by the SNA. Both indices measure value as a bundle of commodities, which is another basic axiom of national accounting.

- Proposition 4.1: the *real value* of a national currency is measured by the volume of national consumption.

The details of this proposition, such as the precise form and content of the volume index, are left aside in order to emphasise the essential argument. We encounter an economic paradox: the value of each individual commodity is measured by means of money and the value of money is in turn measured by means of an aggregate commodity index, but there is no absolute measure of value.

The relativity of value measurement, which troubled Ricardo all his life, is not resolved in traditional value theory. The microeconomic approach ignores the existence of an absolute price and works with relative prices by dividing one price into another, which does not mirror economic reality. Considering money as a mere numéraire overlooks the function of money as an independent store of value. By placing the problem outside the economic realm, the value of money is left to the statistician to determine. Consequently the problem is referred to in rather technical terms, such as 'the index number problem' and 'the quality problem'.

In the next two chapters we attempt to reintegrate these problems into the domain of value theory. While one cannot say that microeconomic theory has not dealt with these problems at all, it has done so in an imperialist manner. It has not given proper recognition to the fact that in the statistics of prices and national accounts is rooted the one and only means of measuring value: empirically. Instead it has assumed that the basic notions of microeconomic theory, such as individual utility, scarcity and marginal rates of substitution and transformation, are operational concepts to which statistical measurement must submit, irrespective of any difficulties in practice. In contrast we consider practical problems as serious challenges to the theoretical concepts in this book, and if a theoretical concept is not applicable within a standard routine of measurement, we consider it useless and in need of being replaced by a concept that fits empirical observations in a better way. The reason for the lack of recognition of the empirical restrictions of value measurement probably lies in the past. The basic concepts of microeconomic theory were invented and used before the system of national accounts came into being, and contradictions appearing in the course of this development were one-sidedly attributed to the younger discipline.

It is interesting to note that the lack of realism in microeconomic value theory has been overcompensated by an unquenched desire for 'real' figures. Idealism in the concepts of theory has resulted in a plethora of empirical concepts for real value, and the development of index number theory is thus characterised by an inventive sequence of euphemistic terms. We have an 'ideal' index, a 'true' (cost of living) index, an 'exact' index, a 'superlative' index and, last but not least, a 'hedonic' index. At the same time the word 'real' is employed in more than one sense in economics. It can mean the opposite to 'nominal', in other words a value figure corrected for a change in the value of the currency unit through a general price index. It can also mean 'volume', which is correction by means of a price index specifically tailored to the aggregate under consideration. It may mean 'material' as in 'real' assets rather than 'financial' assets, or the 'real sector' which produces such assets, as opposed to the 'financial sector', which deals with non-produced assets. In none of these uses is 'real' opposed to 'fictitious', but to the layman the difference is nevertheless unclear.[1] The very act of 'speaking in real terms' conveys the idea that one has happily left behind the cloudy and unreliable world of bookkeeping and institutional regulations, and settled safely in the world of tangible objects. Microeconomic theory prefers 'real wages' 'real taxes', even 'real money' to their nominal counterparts, a legacy of the overriding concern under which the theory was invented, namely to render economics into a hard science like physics, the dominant science of the times.

But the operational issues stirred up by using these terms have not been adequately addressed. To obtain such real variables, nominal figures are simply divided by some notional price index without regard to the ways in which this index is produced and the change in meaning it may imply for the resulting aggregate. Thus it is not by accident that we devote half of the chapters on national accounts to these statistical problems. We will learn about important conditions of measurement for the concepts of the theory of value.

In this endeavour we make every effort to convince the reader that nominal values are real values in the sense of 'actual', and of what is observable as a statistical fact, while real values, as conceived by economic value theory, are constructs. They are imputations in the proper sense of the word, that is, the result of accounting routines based on principles of good practice that require and imply a theory of value for adequate interpretation. The dual character of the national accounts, distinguishing between institutional units and transactions on the one hand, and functional units and product flows on the other, provides the theoretical background for this view.

Looking for authorities to support such a stance, we that find that almost all are on our side if they have not relied on mathematics alone as the tool to solve economic theoretical problems. Ricardo has already been mentioned. Marx had a lot to say about the relationship between business accounting and the theory of value. Marshall and Keynes are known for their preference for nominal rather than real aggregates. Even Hicks, to whom a considerable amount of standard formal economics is owed, was deeply concerned about the limited applicability of his fundamental concepts. Fisher, who initiated what today is called index number theory, never went as far as to attribute to it an existence of its own, independent of economics. At one point or other, each of these researchers became aware of the problems of value measurement, but the reserve that they expressed did not materialise in an adaptation of the inherited concepts of value theory. For a long time the simplification of economic phenomena meant abstraction from problems of content in favour of problems of formal mathematical relationships. It is not our intention here to comment on the history, the hopes, the disappointments and the use and misuse of mathematics in economics. But as stated before, we work on the assumption that mathematics is not a sufficient tool to assure the adequacy of economic concepts for economic measurement.

The new vision achieved in the SNA

The disparities between microeconomic value theory and statistical observation can not be blamed on the former only. They can also be explained by the traditional division of labour that has reigned in statistical offices to date. Value measurement is usually carried out in two departments, each with its own historical roots and specific statistical system. On the one hand the price statistics department collects the details of prices and only prices all over the economy. It is satisfied when it is able to describe their development in a coherent and comprehensive way. On the other hand the national accounts department takes the price indices from its neighbouring department for lack of its own collection unit, and without much concern for and knowledge of the methods and problems involved in their compilation. It is tacitly assumed that if there have been problems, these have been solved by the experts. The price indices are then transformed and adapted in order to arrive at volumes, which is the main field of interest of the national accounts. But the interpretation of the resulting figures is hardly linked to the details of the price observation.

As a result of unstructured thinking, fuzzy concepts develop, such as the so-called 'implied price index'. This is a third-level statistical construct, compiled from price indices after converting them to national accounts uses. By dividing the volumes of national accounts (derived by means of proper price indices) into nominal figures, one arrives at a new price index, now called 'implied'. It is implied, of course, by the mathematics, but the question of whether this may be a spurious implication has not yet been answered, or even asked. The implied price index can hardly be interpreted in terms of the theory of 'pure price change' guiding genuine price statistics. But what kind of price ideal looms behind it is an open question. To date the figure is no more than the residual of a trivial computation.

Overriding the traditional separation of price and value reporting, the 1993 SNA offers a new vision. To quote it directly:

> The System provides a framework within which an integrated set of price and volume measures can be compiled which are conceptually consistent and analytically useful. The primary objective is not simply to provide comprehensive measures of changes in prices and volumes for the main aggregates of the System but to assemble a set of interdependent measures which make it possible to carry out systematic and detailed analyses of inflation and economic growth and fluctuations.
>
> (SNA, 1993, para. 16.1)

Determination of the rate of growth has always been a major goal of national accounts, hence their preoccupation with volume measurement. Now the claim is extended to the rate of inflation, which has been the sole responsibility of the price statistics department up to now. The purpose of the new claim is to integrate the two measurements, and this is new territory for both departments. The two measurements should be 'conceptually consistent'.

Take a famous index number controversy as a demonstration of the implication of such integration. When asked what is meant by volumes, national accountants will usually answer 'Values at constant prices.' This meaning is put into operation through the Laspeyres quantity index. Price statisticians favour constant commodity bundles to measure the 'pure' price movement of an aggregate. This too involves the use of the Laspeyres price index. An integrated system must not use both indices at the same time, because logically they exclude each other. Under the premise that price index multiplied by volume index equals nominal value the use of a Laspeyres index for one component of volume or price automatically implies the Paasche index for the other.

At present the two systems of price statistics and national accounts are carried side by side through our statistical yearbooks. Price statisticians usually publish their indices without any volume figures, so the fact that they contradict the national accounts figures is not apparent. For their part, national accountants mostly publish volumes and some implied price indices, which because of their complexity are beyond the control of price statistics, so their divergence from ordinary price indices is not noticed. This state of affairs is no longer tenable. The SNA calls for integration, and this requires some theoretical groundwork to be done.

It is true that the 1968 SNA claimed to provide for an integrated set of price and volume indices. But it spelled this out only as a model. Based on the framework of input–output analysis, it produced a comprehensive set of formulae for mutually interdependent price and volume indices in terms of matrix algebra. But it never approached the actual measurement process and the conceptual fallacies embodied in it. Even the 1993 SNA cannot go much further, because of its necessarily abstract and general level of argumentation. It is up to the practical statistician to put the integrative forces to work.

In going about the task we make the usual distinction between the 'index number problem' and the 'quality problem', beginning with the first because it is more widely known and discussed. The index number problem addresses the following question. Given the price indices for elementary categories of a product classification, how are they to be aggregated in order to form meaningful variables at the macro level? The quality problem addresses the question of how to arrive at an elementary price index from individual price observations within a certain product group. Keeping the two problems apart is advisable for reasons of analytical exposition, but in the end, of course, the theory must integrate both aspects into a coherent system.

National accounts in nominal values are useful only if applied to the analysis of one nation in one year. Theoretically speaking, they realise the point economy where spatial extension or temporal duration are theoretically irrelevant due to the fact that the value of the currency unit is the same everywhere in an economy, and the time dimension is fixed and taken out of history. These are the conditions of the neoclassical model, where money is really nothing more than a numéraire. It is because money is not an eternally and universally fixed absolute store of value, but varies over space and time, that national accounting transcends the neoclassical model and is forced to develop techniques and theories of value measurement that include the possibility of different values of money. Accounting for these differences transforms nominal into real values.

We begin our analysis of this transformation with the dimension of space because it has commanded less attention among theoretical economists than time, and is therefore less loaded with emotions. We shall not proceed by setting in advance some theoretical goal and deriving the appropriate index from it; on the contrary, we shall take the decision of the SNA in respect of the Geary–Khamis index as given and look for a reasonable explanation of this practically well-founded, we assume, decision and its implications for the theory of economic value.

One difficulty will be hard to overcome in the following two chapters. Both the index number problem and the quality problem command much attention in the literature. It will be impossible to present the current state of the debate here in a way that would be satisfactory to the expert in the field. Many important arguments will be left aside for reasons of simplicity. In particular the debate on the Geary–Khamis index, recommended by the

SNA, and the EKS-index, adopted by the European Union and its ESA, cannot be followed up and decided here. For our purposes it is sufficient to consider the one as an approximation to the other. On the other hand the text cannot be introductory in nature so as to guide the non-expert into the issues step by step. There is a need for compromise, and readers are asked for goodwill on both sides of the boundary of expertise. It is promised that the unusual combination of statistical practice and value theory will lead to some interesting and entertaining questions.

Comparing value over space: the axiom of transitivity

The world on a spreadsheet

An economy is a set of transactions by institutions residing in a nation. The nation legislates its currency. Foreign-exchange markets provide for the exchange of national currencies at appropriate exchange rates. However, while exchange of currencies is easy under conditions of full convertibility, one cannot speak of a world money. There is no overall institutional control of the world's financial system, and no precisely defined monetary aggregate.

In this world of cooperation and trade the economic performance of different nations is compared to that of others on the basis of their national accounts. Each system of national accounts employs its own national currency. Each has its own measure of economic value, uniquely valid and perfectly homogeneous throughout the economy, but invalid and deprived of its uniqueness outside. The theory of value is called upon to explain how the value of different currencies can be compared.

Under the microeconomic approach the answer is quickly given. There are foreign exchange markets. Given full convertibility, the traded currencies find their values on the markets in terms of mutual exchange rates, and if the markets are in equilibrium the exchange rates are the values of the currencies. By applying them to national accounts figures these can be made comparable.

However if the world is pictured as one market and exchange rates as the appropriate currency values, the question arises of why price levels are different in different countries. Equilibrium between markets would lead one to expect that price levels are equal in all countries, and that the exchange rates will be equal to the purchasing power parity of each currency. Empirical investigation has established the stylised fact that the purchasing power theorem does hold in some cases, but not in others (Kravis *et al.*, 1983). So the adequacy, or at least the uniqueness, of the foreign exchange markets as the determinant of mutual values of currencies is challenged. As long as exchange rates do not correspond to purchasing power parity, there are two types of value to be studied side by side – one determined by foreign exchange markets, the other by national price levels.

We begin our investigation by studying the methods employed in the national accounts for the international comparison of aggregates in different currencies. The SNA recommends the Geary–Khamis index (SNA, 1993, para. 16.95), although it also provides for the index formula proposed independently by Eltetes, Kovecs and Sculz (EKS formula, SNA, 1993, para. 16.98). The argument is partly based on technical grounds, as explained in the SNA, but probably also on political grounds, which the SNA naturally does not mention: the United Nations has always favoured the Geary–Khamis method, while the European Union has always worked with the EKS formula. Neither intends to give in. We shall leave this issue aside and discuss only the Geary–Khamis index which has been employed in the International Comparison Project (ICP), organised by the United Nations in cooperation with the University of Pennsylvania, which not only achieved a world-wide comparison of countries on a consistent basis, but also broke a lot of theoretical ground.

Our task differs from that of the ICP in one respect, which is not of importance now at the abstract level of index number theory but will become so later when we consider its interpretation. We look here for a means of determining the value of a national currency in comparison with other currencies, while the ICP is concerned with finding a correct measure of a nation's real GDP. While these two goals are not separate, they are not identical. The difference shows in that here we choose the commodity bundle of private consumption expenditure as the standard of value. We do so because monetary authorities have set this precedent world-wide. Under the ICP, however, the nation's currency is matched with GDP. For what follows in this chapter the difference is not disturbing. The reader may work with any commodity bundle she or he pleases as long as she or he keeps it constant throughout the chapter.

In mathematical terms the Geary–Khamis index is simple.[2] Given a matrix of private consumption expenditure, c_{ij}, which describes the consumption of commodity group i in country j in that country's currency, and matrix p_{ij} for the corresponding prices, one can compile the following:

$$q_{ij} = \frac{c_{ij}}{p_{ij}}, i = 1, \ldots, m; j = 1, \ldots, n \tag{4.1}$$

The q_{ij} are the volumes of commodity groups i consumed in each country, j. The Geary–Khamis rule then defines a vector of world prices π_i for each commodity group, i, by

$$\pi_i = \frac{\sum_j \varepsilon_j c_j}{\sum_j q_j}, i = 1, \ldots, m \tag{4.2}$$

The ε_i figuring in the numerator of the fraction are exchange rates based on the equality of purchasing power between the currencies. They are defined by

$$\varepsilon_j \sum_i c_{ij} = \varepsilon_0 \cdot \sum_i \pi_i q_{ij}, \quad j = 1, \ldots, n \tag{4.3}$$

where ε_0 is an open scaling factor of the purchasing power parities not determined by the system.[3] Equations 4.2 and 4.3 form a system of $(m+n)$ linear equations for the m unknowns, π_i, and the n unknowns, ε_i. They are homogeneous and can be solved if the rank of the system is smaller by one than the number of equations $(m+n)$, which it is. It is the typical matrix equation relating functions (for example commodities) with institutions (for example nations) that is used in other areas of national accounting, such as the double proportional adjustment of input–output tables (the RAS method).

Instead of delving into mathematical properties it is convenient to illustrate the method by means of a small example, too small to have an applicable meaning but sufficient to be thrown on a spreadsheet demonstrating the logical structure. Table 4.1a introduces the initial figures. There are three countries A, B and C, whose currencies are dollars, pounds and francs respectively. Their consumption expenditure is classified into four product groups. In Table 4.1 products are represented along the rows and countries along the columns of the matrix. Thus total consumption expenditure is 100 dollars in country A, 110 pounds in country B and 50 francs in country C. There are no sums along the rows because each value is in a different currency.[4] The conventional method of comparison takes recourse to nominal exchange rates (e). Let these be 2:3:1 for reasons of simplicity. Table 4.1b shows the result. All consumption vectors are now comparable along rows, resulting in a total world consumption expenditure of 580 francs. It may also be expressed as 290 dollars or 193.33 pounds. For the moment the chosen base currency has no importance, serving only as a scalar factor. In order to neutralise the expression completely, it would be appropriate to normalise world consumption at 100, but for reasons of convenience and illustration we shall continue to work with the more handy figures in terms of an arbitrarily selected currency.

In order to check whether the rates at the foreign exchange markets reflect the purchasing power of the currencies, prices are collected in each country for each commodity group. Table 4.2a assumes some prices. It may be observed, for example, that a representative item in product group 1 costs 2 dollars per piece in country A and 2 pounds per piece in country B. Given that 2 pounds exchange for 3 dollars at the foreign exchange, a pound obviously buys more of commodity 1 in country A than in B. The exchange rate is higher than the purchasing power parity. Comparing countries A and C for product group 1 we find that the exchange rate is equal to purchasing power parity.

Hence there is a statistical problem. The purchasing power of money differs between countries and between product groups. If we want to analyse

Table 4.1   Nominal values between nations: conversion at exchange rates
(a) Private consumption expenditure in domestic currencies

Product	Country A (dollars)	Country B (pounds)	Country C (francs)
1	20	35	20
2	10	20	5
3	50	40	15
4	20	15	10
All products	100	110	50

(b) Private consumption expenditure in francs at foreign exchange rates

Product	2:1 Country A	3:1 Country B	1:1 Country C	All countries
1	40	105	20	165
2	20	60	5	85
3	100	120	15	235
4	40	45	10	95
All products	200	330	50	580

these differences, we must define averages that single out the structural from the accidental components of value variance. Equations 4.2 and 4.3 define the Geary–Khamis index for the purpose. They can be rewritten to yield the following system of equations:

$$
\begin{aligned}
32.5\pi_1 &\quad -20\varepsilon_1 - 35\varepsilon_2 - 20\varepsilon_3 = 0 \\
1.17\pi_2 &\quad -10\varepsilon_1 - 20\varepsilon_2 - 5\varepsilon_3 = 0 \\
22.17\pi_3 &\quad -50\varepsilon_1 - 40\varepsilon_2 - 15\varepsilon_3 = 0 \\
11.19\pi_4 &\quad -20\varepsilon_1 - 15\varepsilon_2 - 10\varepsilon_3 = 0 \\
10\pi_1 + 0.33\pi_2 + 12.5\pi_3 + 2.86\pi_4 - 100\varepsilon_1 &= 0 \\
17.5\pi_1 + 0.67\pi_2 + 8\pi_3 + 7.5\pi_4 - 110\varepsilon_2 &= 0 \\
\varepsilon_3 &= 1
\end{aligned} \tag{4.4}
$$

which is solved for

$$\pi_1 = 4.04$$
$$\pi_2 = 56.43$$
$$\pi_3 = 8.71$$
$$\pi_4 = 7.07$$
$$\varepsilon_1 = 1.88$$
$$\varepsilon_2 = 2.10$$
$$\varepsilon_3 = 1$$

In the homogeneous system of equations the scaling factor has been chosen so that ε_3 equals 1. But this has little to do with the actual currency of francs, the chosen currency standard. As stated before, the Geary–Khamis index defines relative values and prices. There is no world currency to serve as the proper denomination of this value. Towards the end of the chapter we will show how this degree of freedom can be meaningfully used to attach the Geary–Khamis system to national inflation measurement systems. Until then we shall use the franc as a preliminary denomination.

Table 4.2b shows the results. Comparing foreign exchange rates and purchasing power parity we find that in respect of the latter the dollar and the pound are overvalued, and the franc seems to be just right. But here the choice of the standard is influential. The franc is just right because it has been chosen as the standard. If Tables 4.1b and 4.2b, the two conversions,

Table 4.2   Real values between nations: conversion at purchasing power parities
(a) Prices of product group representatives in domestic currencies

Product	Country A (dollars)	Country B (pounds)	Country C (francs)
1	2	2	4
2	30	30	30
3	4	5	9
4	7	2	12

(b) Private consumption expenditure in francs at purchasing power parities (real values)

Product	1.88:1 Country A	2.10:1 Country B	1:1 Country C	All countries
1	37.7	73.5	20	131.2
2	18.8	42.0	5	65.8
3	94.2	84.0	15	193.2
4	37.7	31.5	10	79.2
All products	188.3	231.0	50	469.3

(c) Private consumption expenditure in francs at world prices (volumes at world prices)

Product	World prices	Country A	Country B	Country C	All countries
1	4.04	40.4	70.6	20.2	131.2
2	56.43	18.8	37.6	9.4	65.8
3	8.71	108.9	69.7	14.5	193.2
4	7.07	20.2	53.1	5.9	79.2
All products	–	188.3	231.0	50.0	469.3

were normalised at the same total (for example 100), this would show that the franc is undervalued with respect to its purchasing power parity. Another result is the information collected in Table 4.2c. Here the quantities, or rather the national volumes (q_{ij}), have been multiplied by world prices (π_i), which we interpret as world volumes. They differ from the real values in Table 4.2b, except that the row and column sums are identical.

The question now is what the entries in volume mean as opposed to real values. We see here the two sides of the market. One offers value in terms of money and the other value in terms of a commodity. Under conditions of total equilibrium these will be equal, however in a set of purely national equilibria they are not. Thus if for the world as a whole the equilibrium conditions are imposed, real values are equal to volumes for each commodity and each country in total (row and column margins). But within each category there is room for divergence. If country *A* consumes 69.7 francs of commodity 3 in volume as opposed to the 84.0 francs it pays in world money, this must have a meaning. We need to conduct some theoretical investigations.

Three kinds of value

A juxtaposition of Tables 4.1 and 4.2 clearly shows the possibility of employing two different theories of value in an international comparison of national accounts. One option is to accept each market price as it is, be it of commodities or currencies, using the observed exchange rates as value converters. This leads to nominal prices and values. A disadvantage of nominal value figures is that they are just as much an expression of the value of the currency as of the commodity. It is well known that the demand for and supply of a currency are more influenced by monetary factors than by the necessities of world trade. The imputation of purchasing power parities is an analytical device to separate two market forces: those which determine the exchange rate as a store of value (financial forces), and those which work on it as a means of payment (trade of goods and services). Expressing the consumption expenditure of each country in purchasing power units means that monetary factors have been eliminated from the observed nominal values and exchange rates.

In this argument between nominal and real values we have ignored an intricate borderline problem. Countries not only differ in their expenditure proportions, but also part of their consumption lies outside expenditure altogether because it is non-market. Hence the non-market share and content of consumption also varies between countries. We shall leave this problem aside, because in our argument concerning microeconomic value theory the market versus non-market distinction is not relevant, important as it is for the national accounts themselves.

If the exchange rates are considered as the one and only one equilibrium values of currencies (the neoclassical approach), then by definition no other value concept has meaning. The very fact, however, that purchasing power compilations have found their way into standard world economic analysis proves of that such a positivistic view of market variables is too simplistic. We need to extend the theory of value in order to incorporate the results of the Geary–Khamis index (or any similar index for that matter).

The resulting real values are independent of the market exchange rate of currencies. Calling them 'real' has nothing to do with their being more real than the nominal values; on the contrary they are further away from observation. They are imputed by means of the Geary–Khamis transformations. The word 'real' implies that valuation is carried out on the basis that 'a potato is a potato, is a potato', that is, a commodity has the same value everywhere in the world and can thus be used as a control of value against money.

The third type of variable in this context, volume, also reveals relevant economic information. In a country where the real value of a product is higher than the volume at world prices (84.0 as against 69.7 in Table 4.2b and c), this means that the product is relatively scarce in this particular country. Conversely, real value that is lower than volume indicates relative abundance. The Geary–Khamis system allows us to measure scarcity differences, something that microeconomic value theory has never achieved.

It should be clear from the procedure that the Gheary–Khamis index does not define values at the individual level. It defines aggregates, assuming their mutual coexistence and interdependency. It would be misapplied if it were used to explain any particular individual behaviour between two economic agents negotiating a transaction. To make the contrast clear we can say that instead of *ceteris paribus* we work with the convention of *omnibus inclusis*, taking care that everything is included and coherency is assured in the circuit of value through the economy between the nations. We construct what the classical economists called a circuit of economic reproduction.

The aim of describing a coherent circuit of economic flows is reflected in the axiom of transitivity, which governs the whole purchasing power exercise. The transitivity required in the comparison of aggregates between different economies in space means that the comparison does not depend on the choice of a third country as the unit of comparison. A direct comparison, $A \rightarrow B$, gives the same result as an indirect comparison, $A \rightarrow X \rightarrow B$, where X may be any third country within the constructed system. The Geary–Khamis index fulfils this requirement in that it generates a grid of purchasing power parities that are consistent between all countries. The total commodity basket of the group functions as the standard of value for this operation. However, while the comparison is transitive within a given set of countries, the variables generated by the system depend on which countries are included in the system. A Geary–Khamis system of only A and B yields other purchasing power parities than in the system A, B and X, and this might be considered as yielding misleading information. The alternative is to make a direct comparison between two countries, which brings in the EKS index. The SNA (1993) points out that pair-wise comparisons are rarely confined to just two countries in an isolated way. Countries are usually compared not only against each other, but also in all combinations between each other. This leads us to the conclusion that the Geary–Khamis system is the adequate formula, and the EKS system may be used as a practical approximation. Transitivity is required in both.

Summing up our necessarily brief examination of international comparison methods we note the fact that we have arrived at three types of value. The nominal expenditure values are the best known and most commonly used. They imply the conversion of currencies at their exchange rates. Real values, in contrast, are compiled on the assumption of an equal purchasing power of the constructed unit of value in every country, achieved through the deflation of each currency by means of a general price index. Finally, volumes are the result of multiplication with world prices that do not incorporate the average relative scarcity a product may be subjected to in a particular country. They are an indicator of disequilibrium, showing by how much the initial assumption underlying the Geary–Khamis procedure – that of a single economy with homogeneous global markets for each product through all member nations – is not met in reality.

Comparing value over time: the axiom of temporal identity

The historical lesson of the index number problem

Space and time are the two dimensions in which national accounts are compared. Conventional index number theory recognises no essential difference between the two categories of human perception. It defines two abstract situations, *A* and *B*, which are different either in space or in time. The indices used for comparison can be based on *A* (The Laspeyres index), *B* (The Paasche index) or a combination of the two. The theory does not single out a particular index from the many choices possible within the set, and this is the index number problem.[5] Statistically, however, the two index number interests have parted. The measurement of change in time is performed by different people and follows a different pattern from regional comparisons, and our analysis will eventually reveal the way in which the dimension of time is essentially different from that of space, so that the principles embodied in these routines are not interchangeable.

When Laspeyres proposed his index of consumer prices in 1871 the science of economics made a great leap forward. But when three years later Paasche presented his index the economics community almost made the same leap in reverse, and it has swayed back and forth between the two proposals ever since. It is impossible to quantity the effort that has been put into the problem. Fisher's (1927) study became a classic, although instead of deciding between the two formulae he brought in a third, which, Fisher being less modest than his predecessors, he called the 'ideal index'. This sparked off a tradition among authors to attach equally boastful names to their formulae. After the ideal index we had the exact index, the true index and the superlative index. Hedonic indices, although not quite the same, convey a similar message. Between these famous examples a forest of nameless indices sprang up and were cultivated, and a veritable school of index number research developed around the problem as a subject in its own right. But strangely all this happened only in the world of theory (for an excellent summary see Diewert, 1993) – in day-to-day statistics it remained Laspeyres and Paasche indices which ruled the roost, finding their compatibility by practical compromise rather than sharp reasoning, and this being accepted by the public as legitimate. The problem was blown up in theory and resolved in practice.

Whether a solution is actually a solution depends on the criteria one applies. These should not be arbitrary, but should be consistent with the premises upon which the solution is constructed. A conspicuous premise in this respect, underlying all economic solutions to the index number problem, is constant utility over time. Hicks (1940, p. 107f) took note of this, but then ignored it for his treatment and paved the way for his followers. Thus in economic index number theory, production may change and goods may change (although this strains it to the limits), but the map of preferences is stable for infinity. To a layman this premise is not explicable, and it is even less so to a person well versed in the social sciences. It is only understandable as a position of last resort: if we do not assume constancy of preferences over time, then we have no economic theory at all. And the horror vacui of that realisation keeps the assumption alive.

There is also what is customarily called statistical (as opposed to economic) index number theory. This does not make use of assumptions about economic preferences, and thus has more room for manoeuvre in adjusting to reality. Here the originators of the problem, Laspeyres and Paasche, are at home, and this is also the area in which Chapter XVI of the new SNA may rightly be seen as solving the index number problem. Consequently we will not say which index is best, given a constant and consistent map of preferences, because we cannot infer from any observation that such a map exists on the macroeconomic level. However we will address the question of how the problem is solved statistically. In other words we will work without any assumption about subjective utility or implied preferences. As the statistician says: 'A potato is a potato is a potato' as a value measure (Kravis *et al.*, 1983).

The task of the index number studies initiated by Fisher seems at first glance to be simple: to find, among the many formulae on offer, the one which is superior to all the others. In reality, however, the problem is a little more complex. Together the Laspeyres and Paasche indices have the following mathematical property: if they are jointly applied to price and volume indices and are then multiplied, they yield the initial nominal value index. They do not have that property individually. A Laspeyres index for prices and a Laspeyres index for quantities do not match in this way, nor do Paasche indices. As a result there is a logical dilemma. Whatever reason is found for preferring one, the logic of multiplication necessarily demands the application of the other index as well. A Laspeyres index for quantities requires a Paasche index for prices, and *vice versa*. Consequently it is impossible consistently to prefer one index over the other. If, for example, easy interpretation causes one to prefer the Laspeyres index for quantity measurement (values at constant prices), the same is applicable to prices (prices of a constant commodity bundle), but to have both together is logically impossible. The implied negation of its own premise is the logical dilemma fascinating the scholar of the index number problem.

Two options are open for achieving a unique index number formula. One is an authoritative decision to impose a formula by legal act. The other is scientific conviction through reasonable argument. The SNA embodies something like the authority of imposition. If national accountants want to compare their economies they must find common rules, and the United Nations is the agreed body for the purpose. According to this perspective the SNA has solved the index number problem, but this is also trivial. One can also show that there are good theoretical arguments to support the solution worked out in the SNA. They are not all spelled out in the official text, and perhaps they are not even shared by its authors, but they deserve discussion.

We begin our investigation with the following question: in what sense should the required solution be unique? Here an implicit hope of researchers has not materialised. Mathematisation means axiomatisation. As a consequence it was expected that by studying the logical structure of indices one would find some axioms that would be as evident, although at the same time unproven, in economics as those in geometry, and that they would single out the theoretically valid index by mathematical derivation. This hope was comprehensively destroyed by another classic study (Eichhorn and Voeller, 1976). Of the axioms under consideration we can find minimal sets of those which are mutually compatible. But no index conforms to all axioms, nor are any axioms so superior to others that together they could uniquely define an index.

There is an angle from which one might gain a new perspective on this. Eichhorn and Voeller, although belonging to the statistical school of index number construction, are well versed in economic theory. They are less familiar with the actual problems of measurement because they do not work in the field. Hence it may be that some observation concerning measurement has not come to their attention. Let us look at the list of desirable properties of indices that they investigate (Eichhorn, 1978, p. 36):

- Monotonicity
- Homogeneity
- Homotheticity
- Normalization
- Additivity
- Multiplicativity

- Quasilinearity
- Dimensionality
- Internality
- Commensurability
- Proportionality
- Circularity

- Reversibility
- Determinateness
- Continuity
- Symmetry
- Expansibility
- Aggregation

These are properties that an index may have, but none can be said to be so outstanding that it uniquely defines an economic index. In other words none of these properties has an axiomatic character.

We shall not venture into a detailed examination of all these properties. The knowledgeable reader will be familiar with them, and the interested reader will find explanations of them in the literature. Instead we shall pick out just two properties, because they are famous and are important in our context – circularity and reversability.

If q^0 and p^0 are the vectors of quantities and prices in period 0, while q^1 and p^1 are those of period 1, and q^2 and p^2 those of period 2, the value of an economic index, P, for the entire time period is the product of the values of P for the two intermittent time periods:

$$P(q^0, p^0, q^1, p^1) \cdot P(q^1, p^1, q^2, p^2) = P(q^0, p^0, q^2, p^2) \tag{4.5}$$

This is the property of circularity. It is famous because Fisher explicitly argued against it. It was not a property of his ideal index. Nevertheless it has taken a secure seat among the cardinals of index number axioms.

Reversibility is a very formal criterion. It makes sense in the context of dividing an aggregated nominal value into a quantity and a price component. The reversibility of the aggregating function P means that both components are compiled by means of the same function, except that the arguments p and q are reversed:

$$P(q^0, p^0, q^1, p^1) \cdot P(p^0, q^0, p^1, q^1) = \frac{\sum q^1 p^1}{\sum q^0 p^0} \tag{4.6}$$

This criterion has commanded great attention in index number theory, but it has not attained the status of an indispensable axiom.

Returning to the full list of properties that an economic index might have, the new question to be posed in this respect is whether the above list is complete in the sense that it contains all possible properties of an economic index. It seems permissible to look at one other property, which in spite of the ample choice offered in the above list has not yet been considered in the theory, and which might open up a new perspective on the index number problem.

We are concerned with measurement. It is clear that any measurement, be it economic or otherwise, is the determination of a number in space and time. Whatever figure we compile, both its temporal and its spatial identity must be unique. Let us concentrate on the first. If we measure real value by means of a Laspeyres index we employ two points in time: the base period and the observation period. Consequently the result, and not just the scaling, depends on the structure of the base period. The real growth rate between periods 1 and 2 differs with each different period 0 chosen as the base year. Table 4.3 illustrates this. It takes the data from Table 4.1 for country *A*, extending them into a time series of consumption expenditure, with prices for three more years. In principle a Laspeyres index (index at constant commodity basket) chooses the commodity bundle of one year and carries it through all other years as the standard of value up to infinity. The choice of the base year is arbitrary, and yet significant. Table 4.3 shows how the resulting indices of price change depend on the choice of the base

Table 4.3   Comparison of the Laspeyres and chained Fisher price indices
(a) Private consumption expenditure of country *A* (dollars)

Product	Year 1	Year 2	Year 3	Year 4
1	20	25	20	20
2	10	11	13	10
3	50	55	55	50
4	20	23	18	20
All products	100	114	106	100

(b) Prices (dollars/physical unit)

Product	Year 1	Year 2	Year 3	Year 4
1	2	2	2	2
2	30	32	33	30
3	4	7	8	4
4	7	9	7	7

(c) Average price levels (percentage of previous year)

Index	Years 1–2	Years 2–3	Years 3–4	Years 1–4
Laspeyres at				
Base year 1	1.449	1.042	0.662	1.000
Base year 2	1.366	1.017	0.720	1.000
Base year 3	1.356	1.011	0.729	1.000
Chained Fisher	1.407	1.014	0.695	0.991

year. The average price change between years 1 and 2 may amount to 44.9 per cent, 36.6 per cent or 35.6 per cent depending on whether years 1, 2 or 3 are chosen as the base year, and similarly for the price level changes in other years.

In practice the base year dependency has not stirred up much controversy because the monopoly of national statistical offices provides a certain credibility and authority to whichever base year is selected. Nevertheless, under theoretical conditions the choice is arbitrary. Producers and users of the national accounts have long accustomed themselves to this fact, but not without loss of rigidity on the theoretical side. The question is not about the fact that the behaviour of economic agents at time t depends on all times $t -$ i beforehand (causality). The question is about its measurement. Should the height of a triangle today be dependent on whether you compare it to its height yesterday or the day before? The most striking effect of this definition is that real value is identical to nominal value if the base year and the reference period coincide. Is real value then a fiction? Indeed it is, because the correct interpretation of the Laspeyres index is conditional: what would the value of a commodity basket of some base period be today? A Laspeyres index is not a statement of fact, nor is the Paasche index for that matter.

When one speaks of 'substitution bias' and 'new product bias' this is just another way of claiming temporal identity between weights, and price changes. By employing outdated weights, the Laspeyres index does not account for the substitution between goods that consumers put into effect between the base year and the observation year. It also ignores new products that have since been introduced. Calling this a 'bias' implies the judgement that weights should be not outdated but should represent the actual period of observation.

The uncertain legitimacy of the fixed base procedure is articulated and addressed in practical statistics. One says that 'after a certain time' (a typically pragmatic phrase) the base period becomes obsolete and must be replaced by a more recent one, the connection being made by means of chaining. Thus in spite of thinking in terms of constant weights, all indices have at some point or other been chained, the time lag of rebasing being roughly inversely proportionate to the variation of the observed economic change. This is proof that the principle of temporal identity of the variables entering into the aggregates is being observed in practice. Temporal identity means that all data from which an aggregate of time t is constructed refer to this and only this time period t. It can also be called 'base independence' because, by the same token, the aggregate is independent of the choice of a base year.

The SNA's solution: the chained Fisher index

Chapter XVI of the 1993 SNA addresses comparisons in time and in space. For comparison in time the best summary of the recommendations is found in the SNA itself (para.16.73):

(1) The preferred measure of year to year movements of GDP volume is a Fisher volume index, changes over longer periods being obtained by chaining: i.e. by cumulating the year to year movements;

(2) The preferred measure of year to year inflation for GDP is, therefore, a Fisher price index, price changes over long periods being obtained by chaining the year to year price movements: the measurement of inflation is accorded equal priority with the volume movements;

(3) Chain indices that use Laspeyres volume indices to measure movements in the volume of GDP and Paasche price indices to measure year to year inflation provide acceptable alternatives to Fisher indices;

(4) The chain indices for total final expenditures, imports and GDP cannot be additively consistent whichever formula is used, but this need not prevent time series of values being compiled by extrapolating base year values by the appropriate chain indices;

(5) Chain indices should only be used to measure year to year movements and not quarter to quarter movements.

These five statements contain in a nutshell all there is to say about the index number problem from a contemporary point of view. They rule for temporal identity, reversability and equilibrium observation, and against additivity. In the paragraphs preceding this conclusion a careful argument is developed to justify the chaining procedure. Chain indices 'have a number of practical as well as theoretical advantages' (ibid., para. 16.41). One obtains a better match between commodities in consecutive time periods than between periods that are far apart, remembering the fact that commodities are continuously disappearing from markets and being replaced by new commodities, or new qualities. What refers to each individual commodity also refers to their weights in the commodity basket. These too are changing continuously, and a chain index assures that the weights are up to date. Summarising these statements, it seems that the SNA's principal argument in support of the chain index is based on the axiom of temporal identity introduced above. It is not explicitly mentioned, but it seems to lie at the heart of the matter. If one wants to measure a change of variables aggregated by means of weights, and the measure is to be independent of the variables at other points of time, depending only on the variables at the time of observation, or, in practical terms, if one wants the weights to be up to date with the measured price variables, one applies the criterion of temporal identity. Its proper implementation is the chain index in practice, and – to draw a first conclusion – its proper theoretical concept is the Divisia index.

If chaining is the preferred method, the choice of the particular formula to be chained is of secondary importance (ibid., para. 16.30). The discrepancy between the Laspeyres index and the Paasche index disappears in the limit as the time interval approaches zero. It is still there of course, because actual measurement requires a finite period of observation. In the SNA, the Fisher index and the Tornqvist index are considered for the purpose, preference being given to the first. The choice of the Fisher index implicitly reveals another fundamental criterion. The Fisher index satisfies the factor reversal test, or the reversibility test as it is also called (Equation 4.6 above), while the Tornqvist index does not. If

$$Q(p_0, q_0, p_1, q_1) = P(q_0, p_0, q_1, p_1) \tag{4.7}$$

is the factor reversal condition for the one aggregating function Q and P of volume and price, and

$$P^F = \sqrt{P^L P^P} = \sqrt{\frac{\sum q^0 p^1}{\sum q^0 p^0} \times \frac{\sum q^1 p^1}{\sum q^1 p^0}} \tag{4.8}$$

is the Fisher price index, the geometric mean of Laspeyres and Paasche price indices, then

$$
\begin{aligned}
P^F \cdot Q^F &= \sqrt{\frac{\sum q^0 p^1}{\sum q^0 p^0} \times \frac{\sum q^1 p^1}{\sum q^1 p^0}} \times \sqrt{\frac{\sum q^1 p^0}{\sum q^0 p^0} \times \frac{\sum q^1 p^1}{\sum q^0 p^1}} \\
&= \frac{\sum q^1 p^1}{\sum q^0 p^0} = \frac{\nu^1}{\nu^0}
\end{aligned}
\tag{4.9}
$$

satisfies the factor reversal test. But if

$$P^T = \prod_i \left(\frac{p_i^1}{p_i^0} \right)^{0.5(s^0 + s^1)} \tag{4.10}$$

is the Tornqvist price index, with s^0 and s^1 as the expenditure shares, then

$$P^T \cdot Q^T = \prod \left(\frac{p_1}{p_0} \right)^{0.5(s_0 + s_1)} \cdot \prod \left(\frac{q_1}{q_0} \right)^{0.5(s_0 + s_1)} \neq \frac{\nu^1}{\nu^2} \tag{4.11}$$

and does not satisfy the test.

The factor reversal test expresses an idea of symmetry. If an index formula is used for prices, it is logical to use the same formula to aggregate quantity changes. This is required for making the index number formula unique. We have already discussed this point with respect to Laspeyres and Paasche indices. Their logical relationship is such that you cannot apply the one formula (say to prices) without implicitly using the other (for volumes). In a similar way, any other pair of unsymmetric indices I1 and I2 would entail the ambiguity of which of the two to apply to prices and which to volumes. That ambiguity can only be avoided by choosing a symmetric formula for which I1 equals I2, thus obeying the factor reversal test. The habit of looking at only one component and disregarding the implied definition for the other, ignores the logical problem and does not define away the inconsistency of the argument. There is nothing in the concept of quantity and price that warrants a different aggregation formula for each. The axiom of reversibility avoids this split.

A still more stringent argument lies at the mathematical level, and again comes from Eichhorn and Voeller (1976). They show that if you separate a nominal value into two components, P and Q, for which multiplication holds (the factor reversal test) there is only one possible formula and this is the Fisher index. In other words the very construction of a product at the macro level from products at the micro level warrants as its one and only formula the Fisher index. Eichhorn and Voeller do not take this as an index number solution because they do not recognise the qualitative importance of the factor reversal test. However if one thinks about consistency when arguing for a formula for prices and quantities together, the conclusion is inevitable (SNA, 1993, para. 16.24).

If a chained Fisher index is accepted as the solution of the index number problem for national accounts, one major criticism must be dealt with. A chain index does not satisfy circularity (Equation 4.5 above). The same mathematical property is stated somewhat differently by saying that a chain index is path dependent, meaning that the result of the index between two non-adjacent years, 1 and ($n > 2$), depends on the pattern of movement of prices and quantities in the years in between. In the extreme it may happen that prices and quantities describe complete circles, each returning to their original value at time n, and yet the cumulated chain index shows a non-zero difference. 'Even if the prices and quantities for a particular month, or quarter, were to be identical with those in the previous year, a chained Laspeyres volume index could not be expected to return to its previous level' (ibid., para. 16.49). The last line in Table 4.3c exemplifies this property. The chained Fisher index shows a pricel level of 0.991 for year 4 compared with 1.000 for year 1, although the prices and quantities are the same in both years. All Laspeyres indices, on the contrary, show a price level of 1.000 due to their fixed base-year weights.

The factor reversal test was favoured by Fisher, but path independency, or the circularity test, was considered by him to be not only irrelevant but also a false criterion, and this to such a degree that any index formula that was in accordance with it would be considered inadmissible. In other words, to Fisher path dependency was a required property of an economic index. History apart, path dependency needs interpretation today. A hint comes from the practical side. The SNA advises that only situations that are comparable should be chained. Chaining should not be used if it involves 'an economic detour', that is, a comparison of two situations by means of a third that is not comparable to either. Thus chaining seasonal data that are not adjusted for seasonal fluctuations is not desirable, and fixed weight indices would be preferable. Let us add that these fixed weights should probably reflect equilibrium (operationalised by averages) across the observed period. The length of the chaining period should be a year, not 'quarter to quarter movements' (see above), because the year is the natural equilibrium period for the national accounts.

In its remark number (4) the SNA is concerned about the additivity of variables resulting from chain indices applied to variables in the national accounts. Non-additivity is a consequence of temporal identity. It is a problem and needs to be resolved in any theory of value that claims to underpin and interpret the recommended practice.

The Divisia index

As a *mixtum compositum* of the Laspeyres and Paasche indices, the chained Fisher chain index appears to be a quite complicated formula. Theory's task is to simplify practical phenomena, and in this spirit we look at the chained Fisher index from a slightly different perspective than before. We take it as an approximation, on the basis of finite time spans, to an index defined in differential calculus. This is the Divisia index, which is not mentioned in the SNA because it cannot be applied directly to statistics. It is useful, however, in economic theory when it comes to interpreting the results of the procedures. The Divisia index is defined as follows:

$$\frac{dP}{P} = \sum_i s_i \frac{dp_i}{p_i} \tag{4.12}$$

for prices and

$$\frac{dQ}{Q} = \sum_i s_i \frac{dq_i}{q_i} \tag{4.13}$$

for volumes. The s_i are the shares of each commodity in the expenditure vector under consideration. All the variables refer to the same point in time, even those that denote a change in time, an assumption that is made meaningful by the axioms of differential calculus. The formula passes the reversability test, but it is still not useful in this form. Practical use can be made of it through integration. Thus we have

$$P(t) = P^0 \int_0^t \sum_i s_i(\tau) \frac{dp_i}{p_i(\tau)} \tag{4.14}$$

$$Q(t) = Q^0 \int\limits_0^t \sum_i s_i(\tau) \frac{dq_i}{q_i(\tau)}. \tag{4.15}$$

In general the integrals 4.14 and 4.15 do not exist in explicit form. Integration between times 0 and t depends on the concrete functions $s_i(\tau)$, the shares follow in the course of time. The integral is path dependent, just like the chain index. Chaining is thus interpreted as an operationalisation of the Divisia index. Or to put it the other way round, the theoretical ideal for the chain index is the Divisia index. The latter carries to utmost precision the axiom of temporal identity by assigning all contained variables to the same point in time.

There is a special case in which the Divisa index is not path dependent, namely when the shares s_i are constant over time. In this case the integrals of dP/P and dQ/Q exist as the logarithms, and we can derive from 4.14 and 4.15:

$$P(t) = P^0 \prod_i \left(\frac{p_i(t)}{p_i^0} \right)^{s_i} \tag{4.16}$$

$$Q(t) = Q^0 \prod_i \left(\frac{q_i(t)}{q_i^0} \right)^{s_i} \tag{4.17}$$

Price levels and volume aggregates are weighted geometric averages of their elements, or to put it back into index number language, they are measured by the Tornqvist index in the long run. How reasonable is the assumption of constant weights in an expenditure vector? With this question we leave the index number problem and turn back to economic reasoning.

Theoretical conclusions

The relativity of units in economic measurement

The topic of this chapter is how to divide aggregates of transactions (defined in Chapter 2) between institutional sectors (defined in Chapter 3) into a price and a volume component. Having studied the procedures standardised in the SNA for carrying out the operation we are now in a position to reflect on their theoretical repercussions. Concerning the theory of national accounts we have extracted two important principles: transitivity for indices over space, and temporal identity for indices over time. These two principles can be combined under the umbrella of base independence, meaning that a comparison between two countries should not depend on the choice of a particular third country as the standard of measurement, and likewise for a change between two periods of time, which should be independent of the choice of any particular third period to provide the measurement unit.

Both principles stand in opposition to the Lapeyres index, the first index to come into the world. Despite its apparent simplicity, easily capturing people's minds, careful scrutiny reveals that the Laspeyres index is never a statement of fact but a conditional statement. It states a value under the fictitious condition that the base year expenditure structure prevails. Senior as it is, the Laspeyres index requires development and added sophistication, such as that incorporated in the Geary–Khami index and the chained Fisher index, bringing it closer to reality by means of certain principles of observation.

Transitivity means independence of the order of comparison, but it does not mean an absolute value in the sense Ricardo was searching for. The measure depends on the countries included in the system. Dependence is eased when one looks at the world at large, because then there is a certain uniqueness established by history, a given number of existing countries. The member dependency becomes more problematic when it is not the world at large that is considered but subsets of countries. Such regional comparisons arrive at differing results, depending on the grouping. If France and Germany are compared within Europe the resulting purchasing power parities and common price indices will be different from those that would be derived from the global set of countries. The constructed unit of value is not absolute, but it is relative in that it is not given outside the set of countries under comparison, but depends on this very set.

We find here an idea of relativity that is foreign to the notion of measurement in microeconomic theory, created in the nineteenth century, when the natural sciences also believed in absolute measurement units. In this spirit, one is accustomed to quantitative measures being absolute and independent of the object of observation. But the absolute measure of value is non-existent in the national accounts, and acceptance of this fact helps us to understand the national accounts and interpret their figures. There is no physical yardstick (such as a certain amount of some or other commodity, for example gold) that can be transferred between countries in order to measure economic performance in a non-economic, physical way. Comparisons are essentially relative in nature, that is, an individual country or an individual commodity can be compared in terms of volume and price to the average of all countries, but outside this average there is no comparison.

For the dimension of time we have found temporal identity or base year independence of the aggregates to be the overwhelming axiom when compiling volume figures in the national accounts. The chained Fisher index, which expresses this axiom, is even more controversial than the Geary–Khamis index. Temporal identity is inferred as a hidden rule of practice from the observation that in all statistical offices time series of deflated figures are chained if the series extends over a long enough period of time.

The further observation that the frequency of chaining corresponds to the speed of variation of the variables in question leads to the conclusion that the temporal identity of variables – that is, the principle that a comparison between two adjacent periods in time should be independent of the data of other periods – is deeply rooted in statistical practice and calls for theoretical recognition.

Here again we encounter relativity of measurement. Time series of volume and price indices do not result in absolute price levels and amounts of goods produced. The chain index is an adequate measure of change, but it does not (by adding up) determine a level. The change in volumes and prices is determined relative to the current commodity bundle at its present structure and value, which are both variable over time. There is no common physical unit outside the economy that serves as store of the value of commodity bundles in time. The measure of value is relative in time.

In this sense the two principles not only oppose but also refine the Laspeyres index. They attach its basic assumption to a theoretically more stringent choice. For the Laspeyres index expresses the very relativity of value measurement through the arbitrariness of the choice of base year or country. In a form of dialectical perversion, it then pretends to take the arbitrarily selected base as an absolute standard of value for the periods and countries of observation. But when the relativity of value measurement is theoretically recognised, it is also theoretically linked to a more convincing choice of standards. It makes sense to take the total commodity bundle as the standard of value between a group of countries in a spatial comparison. It also makes sense to take the actual values, prices and quantity flows as the standard measure of their actual changes. Recognising relativity of value as a necessary condition of observation helps to formulate it in such a way that this relativity does not fall into arbitrariness.

Comparing the index number systems for space and time, we find an interesting formal difference between the two categories of human understanding. These dimensions are similar mathematically in that there are vectors of classified expenditures, c_{ij}, to be compared. In space all these expenditures occur together, there is the logical relationship 'and' between them, while in time only one vector is actual at one time, implying the logical relationship 'or'. Hence we have no ordering in space, and the transitivity axiom applies, but we do have ordering in time, and the identity principle applies accordingly. The set of consumption vectors is closed in space ($j = 1, \ldots, m$), and open in time ($j = 1, \ldots$) In both cases base independency excludes the Laspeyres index. The computed values depend not on an arbitrary third element chosen for comparison, but on all the included countries in space and the path of development in time. There are some special cases. Path dependence is zero in equilibrium in time, and country dependence is zero in equilibrium between countries, signified by constant expenditure shares, as will be explained in the next section.

Before moving on it is worth mentioning one other cause of relativity that is just as influential as the others. All measurement depends on the classification of goods and services, both qualitatively and quantitatively. The detail into which a certain transaction aggregate is broken down, and for which prices are collected, has a strong impact on the result of the measurement. Here a difficult decision has to be made in respect of gathering comprehensive and precise information, and the cost of its collection. The number of categories and the way in which these are defined influence the outcome, which will become clear when we discuss the quality problem in the next chapter. So-called classification 'bias' is beyond our scope here, but it must be mentioned in order to clarify the relativity of value measurement inherent in the national accounts. Classification is an excellent example of the inevitable interdependency between the observer and the observed object, which is not restricted to economic measurement alone.

Equilibrium between markets

Value theory has to do with market equilibrium, as has the measurement of value in statistics. It therefore follows that the concept of market equilibrium is worth some scrutiny. According to microeconomic theory, general equilibrium is attained when all markets are in equilibrium. The possibility that all markets are in equilibrium but the economy as a whole is not, is not foreseen in this theory. In macroeconomics, equilibrium between markets is the major concern, and the question here is whether the national accounts have information to offer in this respect.

Let us consider consumption expenditure. The aggregate is classified into a limited number (some thousand) of elementary product groups, for each of which the national accounts offer two kinds of information, a value of the expenditure and a corresponding price index. For comparison let us assume that each product group more or less describes a market, in the way this concept is understood in microeconomic theory. Here again we have two variables describing the situation, the price and the quantity of the product sold. Thus, at first sight, the analogy between microeconomic value theory and the national accounts is not difficult to establish. Nevertheless, there are some important differences that stand in the way of simply identifying the two approaches. They concern the concept of equilibrium

In general equilibrium theory an economy is in equilibrium if every market is in equilibrium. Markets are linked among each other mechanically through production and utility functions of the economic agents so that a disturbance on one market automatically affects other markets and their equilibrium. In this model it is inconceivable to have all markets in equilibrium and yet the economy as a whole not. The notion of equilibrium between markets as distinct from equilibrium within markets does not exist.

National accounts, in contrast, have little to say about an individual market being in equilibrium or not. Equilibrium is a precondition of measurement in the sense that reliable data can only be produced from markets that are in a satisfactory state of equilibrium. But the internal structure and dynamics of such equilibrium is below the reach of the national accounts. What they are able to show is equilibrium and disequilibrium between markets. In order to explain we must define what is meant by equilibrium.

In microeconomics a market is in equilibrium if supply equals demand. This being the theoretical definition it is not directly observable. The effect of the condition is observable, namely that prices are constant in an equilibrium market, as the market agents have no reason to depart from their plans and decisions. Thus in empirical economics price stability is the indicator of market equilibrium. How this is measured will be dealt with extensively in the next chapter. Here we simply repeat the result, namely that in the national accounts it is assumed that all markets are in equilibrium. However, there may be disequilibrium between markets and this can be measured, although it is not foreseen in general equilibrium theory. When, in determining an economy's rate of inflation, it is observed that prices rise faster in some markets than in others this is an indication of friction existing between markets impeding the free flow of resources from one market to the other. To take an example: when prices rise in the energy market more than in the rest of the economy funds have not been moved there fast enough to remedy the growing scarcity, it is irrelevant whether this has been caused by shrinking supply or increasing demand. In a similar way when in international comparisons the price level for a commodity is higher in one country than in another this indicates the existence of market friction hindering the free flow of resources between nations.

To conclude, a thorough inspection of the concepts shows that equilibrium is not identical between traditional theory and the national accounts. The gap will even become wider when in the following chapter we analyse the concept of price itself implied in the empirical construction of a price index. For the moment we remain with the formal structure of price measurement, where the national accounts lead the traditional view to a higher degree of sophistication.

The decomposition of value and the problem of additivity

In statistical practice the additivity of aggregates is an important desideratum of an index. The 1968 SNA was proud of establishing an integrated system of price and volume indices within the input–output framework, the main feature of which is additivity of volumes in all columns of use, for example between investment and imports. Input–output analysts and national accountants have incorporated the idea of additivity as a natural characteristic of values ever since. Yet the 1993 SNA challenges this conviction. In recommending chain indices it explicitly opts out of additivity. What can be said in justification?

Additivity means that if two volumes, *A* and *B*, are compared between two points in time and then aggregated this should yield the same figure as when *A* and *B* are aggregated first and then compared. This feature is inherent in nominal values, so it is natural to claim it for volumes and real values also. There is only one index that is additive in this sense – the Laspeyres quantity index – and its historically wide usage has given force to the additivity postulate (SNA, 1993, para. 16.55).

Returning once more to the water–diamond case, we repeat the observation that physical quantities of different commodities cannot be added together. Obviously the additivity postulate is not applicable at this level of physical distinction. The remedy is prices, which make physical quantities comparable and additive. However a problem arises when these prices are decomposed and manipulated statistically to yield further economic information. This transcends microeconomic theory, but it may be useful nevertheless.

In the decomposition procedures for value change over time and space, two additional variables exist between quantity and nominal value, namely real value and volume, both of which have a certain influence on the formation of value. By reducing nominal values to real values one can account for changes in purchasing power, separating the financial from the production part of the market. These real values are obtained from nominal values by means of a general price deflator. All proportions are left unchanged in this procedure, and hence real values are additive just as nominal values are. Additivity has not altogether been discarded from the national accounts in the 1993 SNA.

However it has clearly been discarded from the notion of volume. This may be hard to accept at first, but after some rethinking a reasonable justification can be found. At several points in this book we have interpreted the difference between volume and the real value of a transaction aggregate as a measure of scarcity. Remembering that scarcity is an elementary component of value, we can say that volume cannot truly figure as a concept of value because it does not incorporate scarcity, by definition. Volume is instead what classical economists might have called 'use value'. It aggregates the physical and social qualities of a set of transactions, as specified in an appropriate classification. The different classes of products are distinguished on the basis of their use. It is not by accident that volumes are computed by means of quantity indices. They are no longer quantities in that they incorporate quality, but they are not yet value. They still refer to a certain class of products. Thus it is reasonable to assume that volumes are not additive between product classes. Also, the fact that volumes are aggregated as geometric rather than arithmetic averages fits into this picture. This will become more convincing when we discuss the quality problem in the next chapter.

For the moment let us gather our ideas into a formula. If *p* is the absolute nominal price of a commodity measured as some monetary unit per physical unit, dollars per kilogram, for example, and q is the physical quantity measured in physical units, we commonly represent the nominal value of the transaction, x, as

$$x = p \cdot q \qquad (4.18)$$

The national accounts allow for separation of the various components of the transaction value. We write

$$x = m \cdot s \cdot r \cdot q \qquad (4.19)$$

where m is the monetary factor intervening between nominal and real value, s is the scarcity factor intervening between real value and volume, and r is the quality factor intervening between volume and physical quantity. Consequently real value is given by x/m or (srq), and volume is given by $x/(ms)$ or (rq). Furthermore, if translated into the terms of spatial analysis (Equations 4.1ff) we obtain

$$m = e/\varepsilon \qquad (4.20)$$

which is the ratio of the exchange rate and the purchasing power rate, and

$$s = \frac{\varepsilon pq}{\pi q} \qquad (4.21)$$

which is the ratio of real value and volume of each transaction aggregate. Accordingly, for the analysis of change over time we have

$$\frac{ds}{s} = \frac{dp}{p} - \frac{dm}{m} \qquad (4.22)$$

which is 0 for the vector of private consumption expenditure, by definition, but positive or negative for any other aggregate. Since the volume of consumption has been selected as the measure of the value of money (proposition 4.1), volume and real value are identical, by definition. Any other aggregate following a different price movement from consumption will exhibit a discrepancy between volume and real value change, which we propose to interpret as scarcity in relation to the consumption bundle. The decomposition of value into more than the two components inherited from microeconomic value theory helps us to understand the standard procedures of value measurement in the national accounts, and thus aids our understanding of the economy at large.

Putting the above formulae into words we have
Nominal value = price level * real value
Real value = scarcity factor * volume
Volume = quality factor * quantity.

The last equation will be explained in the next chapter.

The integration of measurement over space and time

The above point is brought out more clearly if we integrate the two index systems for space and time into a single system. We noted above that the currency in which the space comparison is denominated is arbitrary, a true numéraire; or more precisely, as the system of world price indices is homogeneous it does not determine its scale factor internally. This does not mean that we can substitute an existing currency at will. If the comparison uses the franc as its numéraire, country C's inflation will implicitly be represented as the world's inflation. This, however, should be a weighted average of the inflation of all currencies. We must look into the choice of the scaling factor in the Geary–Khamis system more carefully.

From Equations 4.1 and 4.2 we derive the expression for the consumption expenditure of all nations:

$$C = \sum_j c_j \varepsilon_j = \sum_i \pi_i q_i \tag{4.23}$$

If only one period is under consideration, C can be set at 1 (or 100 as index). If two consecutive years are compared the question is what value to assign to dC/dt. It is a change in nominal value, so obviously the change should depend on the change of nominal values of the member countries in the system. Given that $c_{ij} = p_{ij}q_{ij}$ we find by differentiation from Equation 4.23:

$$\sum_{i,j} dp_{ij}q_{ij}\varepsilon_j + \sum_{i,j} p_{ij}dq_{ij}\varepsilon_j + \sum_j c_j d\varepsilon_j = dC \tag{4.24}$$

We also have

$$\sum_i d\pi_i q_i + \sum_i \pi_i dq_i = dC \tag{4.25}$$

By definition, and by evidence, the nominal value of common expenditure should be independent of the exchange rates intervening between them.

This implies that the aggregated rates of inflation are equal to overall inflation, measured in communal prices, and for the real change correspondingly. Consequently we set

$$\sum_{j=1}^{n} c_j d\varepsilon_j = 0 \tag{4.26}$$

Differentials are theoretical tools of analysis that cannot be measured in practice. Translating these equations into the Fisher index numbers, Equation 4.26 becomes

$$\sqrt{\frac{\sum c^1 \varepsilon^0}{\sum c^0 \varepsilon^0} \times \frac{\sum c^1 \varepsilon^1}{\sum c^0 \varepsilon^1}} = 1 \tag{4.27}$$

If the totals of $\sum c^0 \varepsilon^0 = \sum c^1 \varepsilon^1$ are set at 1 in the homogeneous Geary–Khamis system for each year, Equation 4.27 simplifies to

$$\sum_j c_j^0 \varepsilon_j^1 = \sum_j c_j^1 \varepsilon_j^0. \tag{4.28}$$

This determines the scale factor of ε^1 in relationship to ε^0. As a consequence the absolute values of ε^1 and π^1 are determined. The world rate of inflation, P_w^1/P_w^0, is then given by

$$\frac{P_w^1}{P_w^0} = \sqrt{\frac{\sum q^0 \pi^1}{\sum q^0 \pi^0} \times \frac{\sum q^1 \pi^1}{\sum q^1 \pi^0}} \tag{4.29}$$

and world real growth of consumption expenditure by

$$\frac{Q_w^1}{Q_w^0} = \sqrt{\frac{\sum q^1 \pi^0}{\sum q^0 \pi^0} \times \frac{\sum q^1 \pi^1}{\sum q^0 \pi^1}} \tag{4.30}$$

Equation 4.29 defines the world currency, so to speak, as the increase in nominal value caused by price and expenditure changes in member countries. Since the computations are too extensive to present on a one-page spreadsheet it is not useful to elaborate our numerical example in this way. The above formulae may suffice as a sketch of the envisaged integration. The resulting joint system of value comparison over space and time is independent of the choice of an arbitrary base, be it a country (transitivity) or a period of time (temporal identity).

A principle of macroeconomic value theory: *omnibus inclusis*

Relating the concepts we find in the national accounts to value theory, we observe an important distinction. In the microeconomic approach prices, values and factor incomes are defined as partial derivatives. Partial differential changes imply that the two variables in question are the only ones to change – the famous *ceteris paribus* condition known by every student of economics. Empirically, economic change occurs *ceteris imparibus*, of course, so that the determination of partial derivatives requires further assumptions about underlying parameters. Hence arises the opportunity by different schools of economic thought to explain an observed total differential change by a convenient sum of imputed partial derivatives.

National accounts, even in their measurement of incremental changes, employ a different approach. Instead of focusing on a particular action they construct the whole of the economy, represented by its overall aggregates and constructed according to the concept of 'circuit of economic value'. The iron rule observed in all ensuing manipulations is coherency. Variables must add up to their appropriate totals. In this sense the real values of consumption expenditure add up to the same total as the volumes, which is in fact the axiom behind the Geary–Khamis system. Likewise price change and volume change must add up to nominal change for each commodity group, which is an axiom behind the Fisher index. The theoretical picture of this approach is not so much optimality, or rationality of individual choice, but the circuit of economic flows. These flows must be complete and arithmetically consistent, even at the expense of reality, as seen from a microeconomic perspective. Prices, real values and volumes are macroeconomic variables that describe the average state of affairs of the economy. They are loaded with all the statistical problems and errors that measurement entails, but they cannot be rejected or invalidated on the basis of individual information, however specific, concrete and true this may be. It may even happen that variables from the national accounts, if broken down to a certain branch or sub-branch, contradict information collected directly at a lower level of information.

In order to highlight its difference one may call this approach *omnibus inclusis* as opposed to *ceteris paribus*. This means that preference is given to completeness and coherency in the representation of the economy over the specificities of individual behavior. The price indices figuring at the macro level do not explain the price agreed in a specific contract between two economic agents. They are useful only at the macro level, where they explain processes between markets rather than those within markets. And the result of this different view must be a different value theory, because analysing a macroeconomic phenomenon within a conceptual system that fails in terms of comprehensiveness is just as erroneous as analysing a microeconomic event without ensuring *ceteris paribus* conditions. Both views have their truth, but the truth is relative. It is related to the underlying principles of observation, which are different at the microeconomic and the macroeconomic level.

5
The Quality Problem

The index number problem concerns the link between qualitatively different commodity groups. It is handled on the assumption that each group is qualitatively homogeneous within itself, but this is by no means true. In order to arrive at homogeneity the quality problem must be solved first. We touch on an area in which the measurement of value problem is most concrete in that the transactions recorded in the national accounts are gauged to certain goods and services. In this chapter the price observation routines that have become standard in national statistical systems will be investigated in order to analyse the concept of product group homogeneity implied by them. The conclusion is that quality is value. They are the same concept in theory, and are measured by a market equilibrium price in practice. The fundamental notion of a 'pure price change', upon which price statistics rely, is interpreted and contrasted with the price concept in microeconomic value theory. The concept of general price change (developed in the previous chapter) as a monetary phenomenon of value and the reference point against which to study relative price changes of products is reinforced.

The integration of price statistics and national accounts

Vision of the 1993 SNA

As stated earlier, national accounts are usually drawn up in nominal terms, reflecting the axiom that the purchasing power of each unit of the national currency is the same all over the nation at a certain moment in time. Between nations and over longer periods of time the axiom is counterfactual, so means must be sought to account for these changes in order to achieve the purpose of national accounting, namely the comparison of economies over space and time. In fact measuring the rate of growth and the rate of inflation of an economy in a mutually consistent way, as called for in the 1993 SNA, is an issue that has yet to be elaborated and discussed in depth. It demands a new stage of integration of the statistical system of a nation, comparable in its scope to the innovation initiated by the 1968 SNA, integrating national accounts and input–output tables. While the tasks of preparing the national accounts and compiling price indices have traditionally been divided between two separate departments in a statistical office, the two units have now been called upon to work together much more closely (and perhaps to come more into conflict). Thus if national accountants are serious about getting involved in the measurement of inflation, they must fully understand how prices are measured by their statistical colleagues. The textbook theory to which the national accountant resorts for the purpose is not empirically refined enough to grasp the complexity of the price concept as it has evolved over decades of statistical routine and practice. National accountants must learn about the price statistics process in-house. And this needs an understanding of the quality problem.

Similarly, if price statisticians want to become more aware of their internal customers, the national accountants, they must not only be aware of the use that is made of their price indices in the accounts, but also discuss the statistical product that results from the accounting process, the so-called 'implicit' price indices. The latter are sometimes used in a tentative manner, and are even put inside quotation marks to show this. As time goes by and national accountants and the public get used to these indices, the quotation marks will disappear, and with them the only visible sign of the indices' distinction from a proper price index. To the extent that implicit price indices are constructionally and analytically different from explicit price indices, price statisticians should assume responsibility for critically examining them from a professional point of view. The concept of a 'pure price change' is of central importance in this context.

The 1993 SNA and its offshoot, the 1995 ESA, treat the quality problem not in detail but remain on a conceptual level that can be applied universally in all nations. The basic definitions that govern price statistics require an adaptation to be made to the price concept of standard economic theory. On this basis, in this chapter we are able to draw inferences for a theoretical assessment of the statistical procedures considered in the SNA for coping with the quality change problem, namely parallel observation, direct linking, indirect linking, cost estimation and hedonic regression. We relate our findings to the analysis of the index number problem in the previous chapter. Although it is customary, and useful, to deal with the two problems separately, interpretation can only be coherent if the operational concepts are coherent between price observation at the micro level and price interpretation at the aggregate level. This is the microfoundation of economic concepts that conveys operational meaning. Our focus is on the dimension of time, because the quality problem in spatial comparisons has commanded less attention in the literature. Nevertheless a coherent interpretation of the concept of pure price change must stand the test of spatial comparison as well. Therefore we will throw a glance in that direction before finishing the chapter.

Quality composition and its change must be observed at the lowest level of price collection. Consequently we leave aside problems of index number formulae and aggregation in this chapter. We continue to focus on the consumer price index (CPI) as the central measure of price level change. The CPI is broad enough to demonstrate the fundamental concepts of price observation, the other price indices being not essentially different in their methodology. National accountants' view on the issue of quality measurement may differ from the view of those involved with narrow price statistics, because we shall look at economic phenomena at an abstract level while keeping in mind a system of coherent concepts that is suitable for both prices and volumes (*omnibus inclusis*). If we study the quality problem in this spirit, the finding that even at the level of a single individual price observation one measures an element of overall inflation (or deflation), and not just a single commodity value, will hardly come as a surprise.

The task of theory

Before introducing the basic conceptual tools used in the field of price statistics, a general statement is in order about economic theory's role in statistical work. Kravis *et al.* (1983, pp. 25 ff) spoke of this during the third phase of the UN International Comparison Project:

> Without doubt, the rigorous theory of economic cost-of-living numbers narrowly circumscribes the comparisons that can be made. Comparisons of welfare or of costs of maintaining a given level of welfare are justified in the theory only with respect to a given person at a given moment. . . . The theory does not warrant comparisons of the welfare of the same individual at two different times because of the difficulties in assuming that his tastes remain identical as he passes through life. . . . In practice, the limitations set by the theory of cost-of-living-index numbers are generally ignored in inter-temporal comparisons. Problems of interpersonal comparisons are put to one side completely, and money aggregations are simply compared at the two points in time.

This indicates a strong objection on the part of the practitioner to the prescriptions of economic theory. There seem to be certain incompatibilities between theory and practice, and the question is whose fault these are. The relationship between economic theory and economic statistics is often presented as economic theory having priority in the sense that it defines economic concepts, which are than passed on to statisticians for measurement. Economic theory then decides whether the concepts have been well measured or not. Thus it is economic theory that qualifies a concept as true, for example the 'true' cost of living index, and not statistics. Statistics serves only as the executing agent to theory in that its performance is assessed in terms of bias from a true concept developed elsewhere. As a consequence of such false leadership the practitioner generally ignores the theory, as stated above, which is understandable but does not allow for a workable relationship between theory and practice. The statistician ignores theory, it seems, not because of lack of knowledge, but because of too much knowledge. In spite of their in-depth knowledge of reality, statisticians are not given the right to speak about the truth, which would include, for example, the right to disqualify a theoretical concept for being inoperable. We may call this the one-way view of the theory – statistics relationship.

In contrast, a two-way view could be described as follows. The process of constructing reliable and continuous data on economic facts demands great intellectual and material resources. A diversity of facts that goes beyond the imagination of any individual mind is a permanent challenge to the adequacy, logic and cost of operation of a statistical economic concept, and can only be handled by establishing certain repetitive routines. Problems arise *ad hoc* and solutions may be provisional, or even contradictory in themselves, but they are required by the pressure of time and expediency. It is difficult for someone consumed by the daily task of pursuing the rapidly developing economy to sit back and devote energy to clearing up the issues of economic content that arise in the process of constructing the published figures. This is the task of economic theory. From this perspective, economic theory is not normative, but descriptive. It observes and documents the routines that have developed during a hundred years of statistical practice, looks for their possible rationales, and if a contradiction is encountered, sees how it can be resolved, not necessarily by ordering a new rule but by offering a coherent interpretation. From this perspective, no assumptions are made in theory that are not operated in statistical practice. Thus if the assumption of constant preference maps is a reason for making the resulting theory of price measurement inapplicable, as warned by Kravis *et al.* (1983), the theory of prices should be modified so as to eliminate that assumption.[1]

In this spirit, economic theory serves as a mediator between different fields of statistical practice, rather than sitting as a royal judge above them. It recognises that statistics is not a measuring machine set in motion by some superior mind,[2] but an organised division of labour between humans who think for themselves and are forced to theorise all the time while conducting their measurements, so that behind the bare figures disclosed to the public there exists a large body of common and sophisticated knowledge about economic reality, rich in innovative insights and challenging hypotheses that need and deserve to be theoretically supported. This approach is followed in the present book.

An aspect of microeconomic value theory that must be questioned is its concept of price. In standard theory, price is understood as a ratio of units of a numéraire per unit of quantity. More precisely, the numéraire is not relevant because relative prices are what the theory focuses on and explains, that is, the price of one commodity in terms of another. It is worth remembering that this theory is prestatistical – it was established before price statistics and national accounts became a regular government activity. Price theory never became interested in explaining absolute prices, that is, prices in terms of money. Instead the concept of money deteriorated to that of a numéraire, possibly because there was no generally agreed method of measuring money when the foundations of the theory were laid. We shall try in the following section to describe systematically the means of observing what the statistician calls 'a pure price change' in terms of money. If we then connect this to economic theory, it may turn out that the naive and prestatistical concept of price requires some refinement. Related to this are the concepts of value, volume, quantity and quality, which must be investigated as well. Having arisen out of a statistical practice that has been standardised all over the world, they must be incorporated into a comprehensive price and value theory. As in any empirical science, the theoretical questions of what is value and what is price are answered by looking at how they are measured.

One practical difficulty with microeconomic theory is that it does not say anything about quality differences between units of the same product. In microeconomic theory the homogeneity problem is solved by increasing the number of goods and services to any size. If two goods of the same type differ in quality they are different goods. The number of goods can be as large as you please, and this has no effect on the question of equilibrium. Thus if we are not satisfied with the degree of homogeneity of our commodity groups, we divide them into more groups until homogeneity is achieved. Heterogeneity is not a problem in this theory.

In statistical work the analysis starts at the other end. It first classifies transactions into a finite and workable number of categories that are heterogeneous in nature. It than chooses particular items to represent the total of each basic class. An immediate consequence of this is that we do not measure price, but the price level of the commodity group. Although the price of the individual representative commodity is a money amount per unit of quantity, this is not the case for the entire commodity group for which the chosen commodity stands, because the goods in the group are heterogeneous in quality. Not only are goods and services incomparable in terms of quantity units (kilos, metres, pieces and so on) within a commodity group, but they continuously change over time. The homogeneity within the group that is assumed in microeconomic theory must first of all be established by statistical measurement. And the routines of this practice must be studied if we are to understand the kind of homogeneity that results from it. It is definitely not homogeneity in physical features.

The basic concepts and practices of statistical price observation

Classifying transactions

Quality composition and its change must be observed at the lowest level of price collection. It involves an enormous diversity of empirical data. A price collector who visits an assigned shop every month is the first to absorb the information and to classify it into intelligible concepts. One of these is the concept of quality. National accountants may not deal with the quality problem themselves, but they are aware of it. The SNA reflects on this in its opening statement on the topic of quality change: 'Goods and services, and the conditions under which they are marketed, are *continuously changing over time*' (SNA, 1993, para. 16.118, emphasis added). That sentence is followed by: 'In principle, the price relatives that enter into the calculation of inter-temporal price indexes should measure pure price changes by comparing the prices of *identical* goods and services in *different* time periods' (ibid., emphasis added).

The juxtaposition of the two statements raises a question about the logical relationship between them, because goods cannot be thought of as continuously changing on the one hand, and be used for measurement only on condition that they are identical in time, on the other. The two statements, read together, illustrate the essence of the quality problem.

Since some aspects of the quality problem reside with economic theory, as explained above, the expedient way to approach the quality problem is to avoid reference to theory at first, and to begin developing the system of concepts by studying the practice of price observation as it has developed over many years. Although the procedures have converged to some general international standard, every statistical office has its own way of approaching the subject matter. We choose the French way of presentation because it is has an axiomatic touch (INSEE, 1996, ch.1 and annex). In this context 'axiomatic' means, that care is taken to define terms at a lower level of abstraction only by means of other terms that have been defined at a higher level of abstraction, working from the general to the specific in a deductive way. This also creates a kind of ideal. The price statistician will know how often the conditions of this ideal are not met, and ask about the complexities of distribution channels and non-market products in particular. We do not deal with the hard and fast problems of price statistics. Rather we present the elementary case, because here the theory that lies behind price measurement is most easily accessible and can directly be compared with microeconomics. The following is a systematic elaboration of the standard concepts of quality measurement. The reader who wishes to bypass the lengthy argument may refer directly to Figure 5.1, which summarises the definitions.

- Definition 5.1: *the field of observation* of the consumer price index is the set of transactions in goods and services by households, called household final consumption expenditure.

We have couched this definition in terms of the national accounts. In terms of price statistics it reads slightly differently: 'The theoretical field of the consumer price index covers the set of goods and services that have a price and figure in the budgets of households resident in the nation' (INSEE, 1996, p. 8). This definition leans more towards the commodity side than the expenditure side of a transaction. Both definitions are equivalent as far as coverage is concerned, but for the sampling frame it makes a difference whether it is a good or a transaction that is being sampled. We have opted for the latter.

We note the fact that by relying on the CPI the rate of inflation is coupled to a certain sector within the economy, in other words the purchasing power of money is identified with the purchasing power of households. There is no institutionally independent measure for this purpose, an indication that we do not measure an abstract heap of commodities but somebody's transactions in goods and services. It is perhaps no accident that in the case of the CPI the sector to which the value measurement of money is attached represents the total population of a country, all other sectors consisting of non-natural institutional units – corporations, administrations and so on – that exist supra-individually. But households cannot be observed on an individual basis, because there are too many. The information about them must be condensed in statistical averages, established through sampling. This leads to

- Definition 5.2: *classification of households* – households are classified by region, social group and other characteristics so as to represent the population of an economy.

In Canada this is called the target population (Statistics Canada, 1995, p. 15). This corroborates our view that the consumer price index relates to a certain total in the economy, namely the people living and consuming in it, and not the stock of goods and services generated. The household budget survey is the tool of data collection in this area. Worth mentioning is the simple statistical rule that less information is needed for a national index than for indices that describe each of the categories of the household sample.

- Definition 5.3: *classification of expenditure into basic classes of products* – household transactions in products are classified by purpose into basic classes that may be ordered in a systematic way to create aggregates of a higher level.

The basic class of products is the smallest aggregate for which transaction values are collected. This is also called 'basic heading', 'elementary aggregate' or a 'position' (*poste* in the French system). The expenditure of households is classified in such a way that each transaction falls into one and only one class. The validity of the price index depends on the extent to which the households in the survey are able properly to carry out the prescribed classification. The classification of their expenditures provides the weights with which the prices observed for each position are aggregated. They are updated regularly (every year in France, every four years in Canada), so they conform to what is known as a chain index, the empirical approximation to the theoretical Divisia index.

Observing prices

Ideally, in order to ensure consistency between observed price and observed transactions, the prices that relate to household transactions ought to be observed by means of the same budget survey that is used to determine the classes of consumption expenditure. In practice households do not report the prices they pay. They are sometimes asked for quantities, but this allows only rough estimates of the corresponding prices. In general household samples are too small to yield reliable price information, so prices are observed at the places where households make their purchases: the so-called points of sale.

- Definition 5.4: *points of sale* are classified by region and by type of sale so as to approximate the proportions in which the households of the nation allocate their expenditure.

The next and crucial step is to determine a standard that measures value and its change in each of the functional transaction categories. This standard is called 'the representative item' or 'representative commodity' and it serves as a proxy for the whole class of products. It is necessary to represent each class this way, because even with a fine classification of private consumption expenditure there are too many products to be observed individually. For this purpose we must first define 'variety'.

- Definition 5.5: to each basic class of products a set of varieties is attached – *a variety* is a good or service defined in such a way that the full set of them represents the products in the basic class. The terms used to describe a variety are called the characteristics or specifications of the variety.

The catalogue of varieties is the basis for price collection. Consequently a variety must be defined as narrowly as possible in order to identify a price, but broadly enough to cover the intended field of observation. The link between basic class and variety is critical. The one stands for the value of an expenditure aggregate, the other for an index of prices ruling over the expenditure. Their logical interdependence is clear, but in fact the two concepts are applied to quite different surveys. Much of the art of price collection has to do with assuring a satisfactory match between the two variables.

- Definition 5.6: an *item of observation* is a product within a variety whose sale is stable at a given point of sale.

As stated above, a variety must be broad enough to cover the national field of household transactions. Only part of it will be available at a given point of sale. Of this part the price collector chooses a product for which the selling conditions are stable. The product is *bien suivi et bien vendu* (INSEE, 1996), that is, the shop stocks it (*bien suivi*) and clients buy it (*bien vendu*). It is a 'volume seller' (Statistics Canada, 1995, p. 42). The price of this item is registered in the price survey.

The definition of an item includes the fixing of a physical unit of price observation. Price is defined as a ratio of value dimension and physical unit. The market determines which physical unit it is economically rational to use, for example whether apples are sold by the kilo or by the piece, and this unit enters statistical price measurement as a standard determining the meaning of quantity and quality.

- Definition 5.7: an *identical item* is an item whose characteristics are the same as those of the items to which it is compared.

As the item is the concrete object of price observation, it is usually specified more strictly than the variety to which it belongs. The individual specifications form the criteria upon which the price collector recognises the item on her on his next visit. Such details may be divided into those that influence the price of the item and those that do not. Identity refers only to the former, differences in non-economic details do not matter.

- Definition 5.8: a *pure price change* is a change in the price of an identical item observed at two moments of time.

This price change is called pure because it is not accompanied by a change in quality, but beware: even a change in units, such as moving from a four-pound to a five-pound pack, is a quality change under this definition.

With definition 5.8, which is founded on all the preceding definitions, we have arrived at the essential definition for understanding the quality problem. Everything depends on what is meant by identical items. Strictly speaking, items are never identical, and there is even a contradiction between transaction and identity. The price of a non-selling good, for example an antique that is offered in a shop window for some time without finding a purchaser, satisfies perfect item identity. Its price tag may change over time, but by the same token the price is not an observation because it has not been confirmed in a transaction. It is only a potential price. When the sale eventually occurs the price becomes a fact, but the identical good is no longer there. Consequently the regular sale of products, which confirms a price in more than one transaction, requires some qualified identity concept for these products.

The fact that transactions occur in a regular and repetitive way implies that it is not the same physical goods that are traded each time, but pieces that are sufficiently similar to one another to be called identical. We speak of a 'matched sample' of observations, 'which means that they should refer to items of the same quantity and the same, or equivalent, quality in both compared months' (Statistics Canada, 1995, p. 42).

- Definition 5.9: *elementary price index* – the price index of the elementary aggregate (the 'micro index') is the geometric average of the pure price changes observed for the corresponding varieties (ibid., p. 37).

Studies have been conducted on the appropriate form of average, but we shall ignore the latter here because it does not directly relate to the quality problem. The important message is that on the basis of pure price change observation at the item level, the index for the elementary aggregate of household expenditure also reflects pure price change.

Figure 5.1 presents an overview of these definitions. The upper left section shows how household expenditure is broken down into elementary aggregates that are homogeneous in respect of consumption (that is, they are homogeneous in macroeconomic terms) but not at all homogeneous in terms of individual goods and services, as postulated by microeconomic theory. The catalogue of these expenditures is matched by a catalogue of the varieties for which prices are collected (lower right in Figure 5.1). The collection takes place at a sample of selected outlets that approximate the outlets used by households. At each outlet an item of importance and stability in sales is chosen, and its price change is observed and averaged (indicated by $\sqrt{\prod}$ in the figure) between two periods.

It is worth going back to the statistical ideal that this procedure is intended to approximate. Statistically speaking, we have a distribution of price level changes in an elementary aggregate that we capture by means of a purposive sample – or as it is also called, a panel – of price observations. If we want to measure the purchasing power of each monetary unit, the selected items must not be too different in terms of expenditure weights. The selection of points of sale should also follow the expenditure pattern. It is difficult, however, to assign actual weights to the items because that would entail a complete classification, where each transaction is allocated to one and only one item. At the micro level of observation this is not feasible.

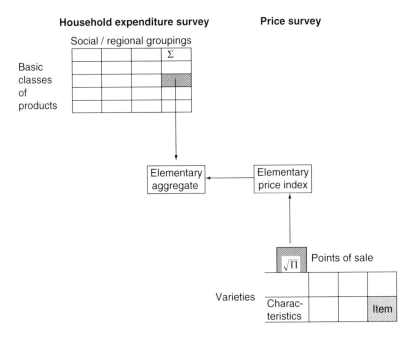

Figure 5.1 Stratification of the price index sample

The lesson to be learnt from this brief but systematic exposition of the CPI measurement system is twofold. The common assumption that for every price index there is a complementary index of quantity is applicable at the level of the elementary aggregate or basic class, because here we have information about prices and values, two of the three considered variables. It is a macroeconomic concept. But at this level products are heterogeneous, so the quantity concept is not meaningful by itself. Where products are homogeneous at the level of items, neither quantity nor value information is available. The item is representative only for the price it carries from one period of observation to the next in its function as a store of value.

To summarise, let us return to the two seemingly contradictory SNA statements introduced at the beginning of the section, concerning the qualitative identity of items in a continuously changing commodity world. Measurement of inflation does not require that items remain identical throughout the reporting period, for example 20 years. On the contrary, this is required only for the time interval between two price observations, for example one month because we sample not prices but pure price changes, and the sample must vary with time in order to be representative. A sample of this sort is usually called a panel. It loses items and incorporates others needed for representability. Thus the birth and death of commodities in the sample is not conceptually contradictory to the required qualitative identity. This is required only over the finite time period needed for the practical observation of change. This interval approaches zero in its mathematical limit, similar to the way in which velocity is measured between two discrete moments in time, although conceptually it is defined for one moment only.

Drawing a fresh sample of representative commodities for every observation period is out of the question, of course. It is preferable to stick with an item as long as possible, not for theoretical reasons but because of the costs involved in a perfect sampling procedure. Sampling prices every time an observation is made would incur prohibitive costs. Also, bringing in more samples would not automatically reduce sampling error. The increased number of observations might be outweighed by an increase in variance, and this is to be expected in price statistics, with its enormous diversity of products. In any case, maximising the life of an item in the sample, or as we had better say, in the panel of observation, is a practical, not a theoretical requirement.

The representative commodity

Three basic methods of working a price panel

The techniques at hand for replacing an item of price observation in the panel are briefly described and commented in the 1993 SNA. We introduce them here one by one, and discuss them against the background of the question about the meaning of quality change and qualitative identity.

Parallel observation (called 'splicing', Statistics Canada, 1995, p. 95)[3] is the first of these techniques and means that before one item is replaced by another the prices of both are observed in parallel for at least one period of time. The logarithm of the price index over time first sums the logarithmic price changes for the outgoing item, and continues with the price changes for the incoming item. Figure 5.2a shows this by means of squared price quotations for the outgoing item and circled quotations for the incoming item. The squared item is followed from t_0 to t_3. At time t_3 the prices of both items are observed so that for the price change over the next period the circled item can take over. The measured variables are not the prices themselves but their changes, as represented by the arrows. In a more refined way, one would observe both items over more than one period of time in order to even out volatility.

The method of splicing is based on the implicit assumption that the difference in the market price of the two items (or the two outlets) is entirely attributable to quality differences between these items (ibid.) In other words, under certain conditions it is the market that measures quality. Splicing requires the two items under consideration to be observed side by side for at least one period of time (overlapping observations). If not the second

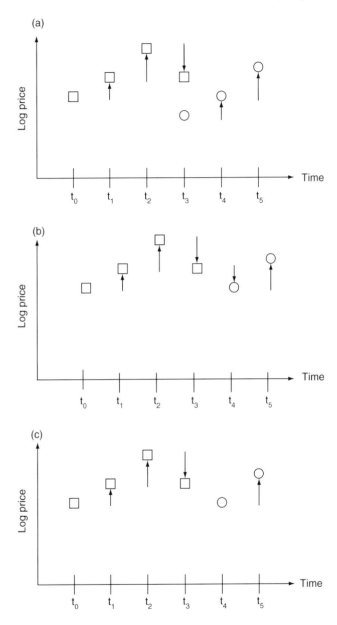

Figure 5.2 Different ways of replacing items in a price panel

method of item replacement may apply, called direct price comparison[4] (Figure 5.2b). The price of the incoming item continues the price series of the outgoing item without an adjustment for quality difference, as signified by the arrow at t_4. The SNA (1993, para. 16.119) recommends against this technique, arguing that ignoring changes in quality is likely to introduce 'serious biases of unknown size, or even direction' into the measured price indices. However there are circumstances in which the technique may be used. If items are not identical in terms of characteristics but are equivalent, unadjusted linking is permissible (INSEE, 1996). Quality change is not ignored but is judged as being either non-existent or at least economically insignificant. The conditions under which this can be done must be specified of course.

Finally, if two items cannot be considered equivalent the third method of replacement applies, which is 'to omit the item in question and not compile a price relative for them' (SNA, 1993, para. 16.118). One series ends and another is started without a connection being made between them (Figure 5.2c). It is the only available technique when there is no information about the quality relationship between the two items. And just as in a relay race, if the stick is not passed on the race stops – a lost item does not add information to price statistics. In practice one imputes the average price change for the aggregate to the item in question in order to maintain the series, but that is no different from dealing with a general change of item in the panel. The SNA recommends against this technique on the ground that it diminishes the comprehensiveness of price observation, which is true. But it is unavoidable and must be shown and acknowledged as a fact of measurement if primary information is to be distinguished from derived averages. As we have argued before, the fact that items change in the sample cannot be objected to on theoretical grounds; on the contrary, such changes are required for updating. The loss of an item adds to measurement error because it reduces the size of the sample, but that cannot be remedied other than by an increase in sample size. Instead of trying to suppress this statistical fact by imputed quality adjustments it may be wiser to report an estimate of sampling error, and thus to educate the public about the intrinsic relationship between statistical precision and the economic cost of a measurement system.

These three techniques – splicing comparable items, direct comparison of equivalent items, and discontinuation of outdated items with the introduction of new items – exhaust the logical possibilities of working a price panel over time, but there are some techniques used in practice that approximate them. In this case prices are not observed but estimated indirectly from other information.

Approximative techniques

One such possibility is to use the estimated relative costs of production as estimates of their relative prices, and hence their relative qualities (SNA,

1993, para. 16.124). For this purpose a standard commodity is constructed that may or may not be actually sold on the market, but its components are, so that the cost of the standard is derived as the sum of costs of the components, a technique used for buildings, for example, but which can also be applied to non-market output such as health services. The SNA calls this an indirect method, which implies that the first method of observing parallel sales is seen as a direct measure of quality.

An extension of this indirect method is the hedonic hypothesis. Here the different components are not additive but are subject to a more general algebraic function of the characteristics specifying the variety. The idea is that if a specification completely describes the variety, then any change in quality must be traced back to a change in an element of the specification. The SNA explains its principle with great simplicity. Suppose, for the purpose of argument, that the prices of different items of a variety are a function of only one characteristic, such as size. Suppose further that the following sizes are on sale in two periods of time, 0 and t:

Period 0	Period t
s_1	s_3
s_2	s_5
s_4	s_6

In this extreme case no size is sold in both periods so a comparison of identical items is not feasible – the price series would break down. However, by calculating the regression of price on size in each period it is possible to obtain estimates through interpolation of the price of size 3 in period 0 and of size 4 in period t. Even an estimate for sizes 1, 5 and 6 may be possible through extrapolation. Joining the computed prices to the actual prices allows price changes to be estimated in the absence of direct comparisons. This so-called (and misnamed) hedonic hypothesis may be used for any goods or services whose prices depend mainly on a few basic characteristics that are easily quantifiable and of which sufficient combinations or qualities are on sale at the same time.

This completes the range of options offered by the SNA for dealing with the quality problem in price comparisons over time. It is not exhaustive. Statistical offices have been inventive in this field, but we shall not delve into this here. Instead a few theoretical remarks are in order. Firstly, given the importance the quality problem assumes in practice, these few deliberations do not solve the practical problem of determining quality change, which is a never ending task anyway. However they are sufficient to bring in a national accounts point of view on a problem treated in practice only by price statisticians. Secondly, if the order in which the techniques are presented in the SNA is indicative of preference, then the splicing technique is preferred, in which case the other methods are not alternatives but auxiliary techniques that are implemented when less than the required parallel information is available. Thirdly, and most importantly, the prominence accorded to the splicing technique implies that quality is measured by the market. There is a qualification, of course, which is that the market must be properly functioning. But if it is, price measures quality.

The meaning of quality and qualitative identity

It seems we have ended up with a logical circle: we measure a price change by means of identical items, and whether items are identical is signified by their price. We need to construct our logical measurement system more carefully to resolve this conundrum. In this respect we receive help from the ESA, which details some of the issues raised by the treatment of the quality problem in the SNA.

Following definition 5.8, a pure price difference in time is observed for two identical items. Items are deemed identical if they are identical in all characteristics that are economically relevant. The SNA stresses that the quality of a product pertains not only to its physical characteristics, but also to all the social and economic circumstances of its production, distribution and consumption (ibid., para. 16.107 ff). Thus a different point of sale means a different quality, and prices cannot be directly compared. Or, if in the course of its life-cycle, a product appears on the market at a high price, carries a medium price when it has become popular, and phases out at a low price, the first and the third prices reflect quality differences in respect of what is considered the normal price that the good fetches in between. On the other hand, even conspicuously different physical qualities do not necessarily matter, the colour of a shirt for example. A red shirt may sell for the same price as a blue one. It all depends on whether differences in quality are economically significant and influence the market price.

The market determines the characteristics that determine a commodity. The statistical task is not to decide what is quality and what is not, but to identify what market participants believe, and demonstrate in their reactions. An identical item, then, is what is accepted as identical on the market. It is a store of value through time and strong enough to check the value of money given for it in exchange. Obviously the market must be well-functioning in order to produce such information.

The ESA elaborates on this point: 'The existence of observed unit value differences is not to be considered as an indicator of differences in quality when the following circumstances apply, namely lack of information, price discrimination reflecting limitations in the freedom of choice and the existence of parallel markets. In these cases, the unit value differences are considered as differences in price' (ESA 1995, para. 10.19). The three conditions specified in the ESA are relevant for determining whether a market is in equilibrium. Lack of information is obviously an obstacle to the functioning of a market. Put more precisely, the notion of price as a social norm is based on the existence of a communications network that reproduces itself independently of individual participants. Lack of information causes prices to differ for the same commodity, and in that case the average is an appropriate measure to estimate the point of gravity. On the other hand it follows, although this is not stated in the ESA, that if the market is so narrow that nobody is informed about other sales, the notion of price is inoperative and must be discarded altogether as a means of measurement. Price discrimination goes one step further in that the buyer or seller may know about differing prices, but are not in a position to take advantage of that knowledge. Their freedom of choice is restricted. Again such price differences do not constitute differences in volume but in purchasing power or 'pure price'. Finally, in parallel markets information is open and choice is unrestricted, but supply or demand are restricted. As a consequence a second market opens up where the excess demand or supply are satisfied, usually with some institutional flaw, and again, according to the ESA, the unit value differences do not indicate differences in quality but in the purchasing power of the means of payment.

Economic significance is determined by markets. Its essential determinants are contained in the classification and description of basic classes and their varieties. This formal knowledge is refined by market expertise, which allows one to ascertain whether or not there is qualitative identity. In conclusion, qualitative identity means economic identity.

This brings in the second criterion for the choice of a representative commodity: besides being identical it must be important within its class of transactions. Even if two items compared in two adjacent periods are identical, the comparison is impaired if an item cannot be regarded as sufficiently typical in one of them. Rigorously stated, the conditions upon which price comparison is based are that the representative commodity is economically identical and important in both instances. If the representative commodity is both identical and important it is permissible to employ the macroeconomic principle upon which price comparisons are based: 'The assumption that changes over time in the price of peas represent price movements of tinned vegetables is basic to price index construction'. (United Nations, 1992, p. 29). This can be called the principle of extension, which means that the price of the item observed at the microlevel can be generalised as an indicator of a general price index within the total expenditure class in question. It also implies that a price index formed in this way can be divided into the expenditure total, to yield a meaningful variable of the total. These products being heterogeneous – tinned vegetables, for example, instead of peas – the resulting variable can hardly be called a quantity. Rather it is called a volume, which can be interpreted as a product of quantity and quality.

Qualitative identity and difference are determined by the market and assessed by the expert statistician, be it at the point of price collection or at the office during the construction of variety specifications. There is an obvious problem with this system, although not often mentioned, in that price comparison breaks down when there are no items that are identical and important, so that in theory there is no quality problem. Either identical items exist or they do not. The problem of quality arises in the empirical application, where an item may be identical but not important in both periods, or the other way round. A lot of *ad hoc* rules are applied in this area, which we are not concerned with here, interesting as they may be as realisation of the qualitative identity concept.

Some formal principles can be inferred from our investigation of the quality problem that are related to the index number problem in the previous chapter. When in the comparison of time we construct a times series of matched samples, we find path dependency. This can be illustrated by means of a standardised example. When nylon was invented, cotton shirts were in widespread use and also served as the price representative of shirts. As demand and technology developed, cotton shirts went out of fashion and were devalued, the wash and wear quality of nylon shirts commanding a superior price and acceptance on the market. As demand and technology developed further, cotton shirts disappeared and nylon shirts became the price representative. The change from the one price representative to the other was noted as an improvement in quality (no price change). A decade later, health concerns and new marketing brought back the cotton shirt. This time it overtook the nylon shirt in price. Again this is rightly interpreted as an expression of higher quality, although in physical terms we are back at the original state. In this way the matching of items within a basic class of transactions corresponds to the matching of weights between these classes for the same reason of temporal identity. All variables should be extant during the same period of observation, and not taken from some other period, the so-called base period.

If in the microeconomic understanding of value theory the value of a transaction is explained by the quantity of a commodity sold and its price – value = quantity × price – national accountants and price statisticians prescribe a different order. Here it is the value of transactions within a commodity group that is given and the quantity component, or the volume as it is better called, is derived from it on the basis of the measured price level in the group, namely volume = value/price index.[5] This volume may increase for two reasons: because greater quantities of the same goods within the commodity group have been sold (this is the usual but most unlikely interpretation), or because more goods of higher quality and higher price have been sold than before, and fewer goods of lower quality and lower price. If there is a measure of quantity for the product group, we may extend the sequence of definitions to quality = volume/quantity. This definition of quality depends on the quantity dimension chosen (pieces or weight) and the aggregation level. The triple concepts of volume, quality and price, defined at the elementary aggregate level, stand in contrast to the dual world of quantity and price pictured in microeconomic theory. They can be reconciled if we reintroduce into the theory of value the concept of the value of money (see Chapter 7).

The type of homogeneity that plays a role in national accounts is different from that in microeconomics. The homogeneous good is used in order to define a price change. Given this price the resulting deflated value within a category of goods is anything but homogeneous. In other words volume in the national accounts is unhomogeneous, as opposed to quantity in microeconomics. At close scrutiny we notice that even for the price representative the concept of a homogeneous good is not realised in an absolute way. When an interviewer enters a store and looks for the commodity he or she registered last time, his or her memory serves to identify the commodity. But knowing that the commodity will not be the same one because it has been sold or discarded, he or she looks for another commodity that is most like it. The interviewer is helped by a certain commodity specification, which defines the characteristics of the product that are economically significant under conditions of equilibrium. However this cannot be relied on completely because specifications must leave room for interpretation, and even the most concise specification may itself experience a rise or fall in value. So knowing that the former commodity is not there the interviewer makes a judgement about quality. He or she is perhaps happy to be able to confirm the absence of quality change, but of the estimation of quality he or she is not spared. And the judgement is about the relationship between the observed price and the underlying economic quality, or as we may say again, value. Price statisticians struggle with a distinction essential to their task, namely the distinction between value and price, a distinction known to the classical value theorist but overruled by microeconomics. Agreeing that the quality of a product is nothing but value, in this sense measured by but not identical to the market equilibrium price, is a first step in reconciling modern statistical practice with the traditional theory of value.

Price comparison in space

The same applies to a panel of items used for comparison in space. We shall take a brief look at spatial quality comparisons in order to consider the same problems from a different perspective. Instead of removing or bringing in an item we have the problem of items not being found in all countries. Instead of splicing we have linkage. When an item is found in countries A and B and another item in countries B and C, the comparison between A and B is made on the basis of the quality difference between the two items, as determined by the price difference in country B. Direct comparison is also feasible, especially when one looks directly for the volume seller (of beer, for example). And finally when a comparable item is missing for a product group instead of the missing price quotation the average of all is inserted into the time series.

According to the *International Comparison Handbook* (United Nations, 1992, p. 34) if items are to be deemed identical:

- the units must be the same;
- physical properties that may have a significant influence on the price must be the same;
- the types of outlet must be the same;
- the delivery conditions must be the same.

This is summarised by the following statement: 'the principle of identical items means that there should be no difference in either the quantity or the quality of the specifications selected among countries that significantly influence the use of a given good or service' (ibid., p. 31). On the other hand, within a country, or even between countries, the 'potato is a potato is a potato' principle is evoked: 'For a large number of consumer items prices vary greatly by outlet and region and between rural and urban areas. But the item should be the same nation wide.... The comparison based on the national average price of potatoes does correctly reflect the cost of resources involved in each country in getting a kg of potatoes to consumers'. (ibid., p. 34). Here it seems that conditions other than physical ones, do not matter. And in fact the equivalence in use principle 'is generally not adopted in ICP' (ibid., p. 51). Now we are caught in a contradiction.

In this spirit the *International Comparison Handbook* resolves that 'The first choice for countries is to price identical goods and services. However, countries must remain prepared to question the obvious identity of brand with brand or a first class ticket in one country with a first class ticket in another. These questions should be raised with regional co-ordinators or in meetings with pricing counterparts in neighbouring countries' (ibid., p. 53). Identical-ness is thus perceived first of all in terms of language: 'first class' here and today is identical to 'first class' there and tomorrow. This is the basic hypothesis up on which we must rely in our daily communication and exchange. But we are prepared to justify critical cases.

The question is how much this theoretical requirement can be relaxed for statistical purposes. 'It is often necessary to trade identity (e.g. brand names) for importance to make sure that items are characteristic of the purchase of a country in a basic heading' (ibid., p. 30). Sometimes importance is even put into the specification, such as the 'local volume selling beer' (ibid., p. 53). It is interesting to ask why such a specification would not occur in a time comparison. The reason seems to be that the local markets for beer are separated. Assuming that equivalence in use is given, exemplified perhaps by travelling expatriates who drink beer wherever they find it and thus carry an implicit standard of value ('basic needs') around the world, the 'beer is beer is beer' principle can be applied and representativeness can be maximised. In a comparison over time on a national market, different brands compete, and if they run side by side in equilibrium they may reflect a quality difference in their prices.

The same is true for comparisons in space. If in a comparison of three countries, two countries have no common item but each has a different item in common with a third country, the price difference between the two items in the third country determines the quality difference between the items, which is exactly what the Geary–Khamis formula would prescribe, extending the principle of transitivity to this level of operation. The same bundle of goods is used as a standard of value in all countries.

Quality and price

Microeconomic theory incorporates the assumption that quality and price of a good are two distinct variables that can be measured independently of one another. All elements of quality are contained in the good which is homogeneous in time so that quality is observed implicitly by the quantity of the good. It is not really measured. If two goods are different in quality to a degree that it affects their price they are redefined as belonging to different classes of goods. This is not in conformity with everyday knowledge, and less with price statistics and the national accounts. The detail with which the rules of price measurement have been explored in this chapter is sufficient to prove the discrepancy that exists between the concepts employed in the two areas of economics, concepts that are different even if they travel under the same name. Let us summarise the findings.

First there is a difference in the way prices are looked at. In microeconomics prices are visualised as relative, that is they are relationships of value between different goods, no concern being given to the means through which these prices are realised, money. In price statistics, however, it is the absolute price that counts, and if a relative price is derived, this refers to change either in time or in space within one and the same commodity group. Relative prices between goods are not observable. This is best illustrated by the fact that for any base year that is chosen prices are always 1 or 100 percent for all commodities, and only the ensuring changes are comparable.

Secondly, the meaning of the concept of price itself is different in the two fields. What is called price, more precisely pure price, in the field of price statistics, does not even exist as a concept in microeconomics, as it refers to the purchasing power of the means of payment in operation. It has been shown in this chapter how much care is taken in price statistics to single out the pure price change from the total price change observed on a market. Every influence related to the commodity or product of the market must be excluded, not only physical changes but also institutional changes that respond to changes in the pattern of supply or demand. In other words if a pure price change is observed under conditions of ceteris paribus, then in terms of the microeconomic language neither the supply function nor the demand function have moved.

This entails thirdly that any variable contained in these functions not being captured by a pure price change by definition, it must flow into the quality change, this being the logical complement to the pure price change. Hence we arrive at the statement that what is price in microeconomics is quality in price statistics. The quality of a good is measured by its price.

Fourthly and lastly, quality is part of volume of an aggregate so that what is price in microeconomics is incorporated in the quantity component of aggregates of the national accounts. Price and quantity cannot be disentangled at the macroeconomic level. They are not observable variables for the national accounts. As a consequence functions of supply and demand cannot be applied as easily as in microeconomics. In fact they do not really touch the macroeconomic realm, because in the national accounts one must a priori assume that equilibrium within markets, where these functions apply, has been attained in order to make values and prices observable. Thus the value concepts of the macrolevel are different from those of microeconomics, but they do not contradict them. While it is still useful to explain market behavior in traditional terms of microeconomics, it must also be realised that these concepts have a limited range of application and are misleading when applied to variables defined by means of national accounts. In the last part of this book we will investigate the relationship between national accounts and value theory in depth.

Part III
Theory of Value

6
Elements of Value Theory

In Part III of this book we draw on the analysis of national accounting principles conducted in Parts I and II. The subject matter of this chapter is the distinction between the microeconomic approach and the macroeconomic approach to value theory. Each approach is presented in its axiomatic form, and the differences and contradictions between the approaches are pointed out.

Preparing the ground for the macroeconomic–microeconomic contrast

It is clear from the preceding chapters that national accounts are about economic value. They deal with this concept in many ways even where they do not call it such, but quality. It has also been noted in several places that microeconomic concepts of value theory are not applied. So the question arises of whether there are two theories of value, one microeconomic and the other macroeconomic in approach, and if there are, whether they can exist side by side, one being used for economics and the other for the national accounts.

What is value theory? Let us begin by clarifying the terminology. By 'value' we mean economic value: value that is circulated, accounted for and stored by means of money. This does not deny the legitimacy of using the word in a different context, for example in game theory, but this is how we understand it here. And what we mean by 'economic' as opposed to other kinds of value (moral or social).

As a topic in the economics literature, 'value' has become rather uncommon. The last three books added to the library at the University of Cambridge under the title 'Theory of Value', for example, were Debreu (1959), Abraham-Frois and Berelli (1976) and Horvat (1995). Hence a volume has appeared approximately every 20 years, enough to keep the topic alive perhaps, but not to make it popular. Horvat calls his book 'a new approach', asserting that neoclassical economics explains value by reference to scarcity, and that this is a tautology because scarcity is also measured by price. Moreover the schism of the economics discipline into the micro and macro branches needs to be overcome, requiring a new paradigm for a single economic science. The new paradigm is a labour theory of value purged of its errors of the past and put into modern mathematical guise. This is akin to the stance taken in this book, except for its complete disregard of statistical practice. Twenty or so years ago Abraham-Frois and Berelli (1976) described their theory of value as 'a mathematical integration of Marx, von Neumann and Sraffa'. This too was a quest for unity, though in a different guise.

Gerard Debreu (1959) characterised his theory of value as 'an axiomatic analysis of economic equilibrium'. An axiomatic approach is usually attempted when a theory is complete and distinct in respect of its propositions, so that these can be reorganised into a coherent and logical set. It indicates that the theory has reached a state of maturity. In this sense Debreu's book marked the initiation into adulthood, and the coming to power within the profession of a theory that had arisen some generations earlier under the flag of 'marginalist revolution'. The book has become a cornerstone of microeconomics, and we take it as our point of departure.

In the early 1970s there was considerable debate on value theory. One of the most lucid texts came from the Socialist world and was called *Proportions, Prices and Planning* (Bródy, 1970), indicating that the intricate relationship between prices and quantities was not realised by the partial equilibrium of individual markets, but by adjusting the sectoral proportions of an economy.

Returning to our original question – what is value theory? – we note that Debreu's book was the last one in the economics mainstream to include 'theory of value' in its title. We can now find 'theory of the household' and the 'theory of production' in our elementary textbooks, or 'general equilibrium theory' for those who long for more. The very term 'theory of value' has been abandoned by the mainstream, being kept alive only by the critics. This prompts a hypothesis. Could it be that microeconomics is no longer concerned with the explanation of economic value, as it was in its early days, but has grown into a general theory of behaviour, including, if you will, political and other social sciences?

If this is so, then we have no economic value theory at the moment. More precisely, since it is not possible to have economics without value theory, the official value theory still has a function and a name, but it is no longer effective, while a new theory of value is being used piecemeal under a different name, the 'national accounts'. We may be at the point where the national accounts take over the task of defining and explaining economic value from general equilibrium analysis, as the latter turns to larger, non-monetary concerns and applications.

For an illustration of this developmental hypothesis, consider Figure 6.1. From the beginning of classical economics, dated here as the temporal coincidence of the appearance of a great book and a great revolution in

1776, we can see two strands of thought developing: the marginalist school, exemplified by the appearance of Walras's *Elements de l'economie politique pure* in 1874, and Keynes' *General Theory of Money, Interest and Employment* in 1936. The marginalist ideas were refined and developed into general equilibrium theory, of which Debreu's book was a milestone. Keynes was followed by the neo-Ricardians, and here Sraffa's book *The Production of Commodities by Means of Commodities* (1960) is pertinent, together with Bródy (1970) writing from a Marxist point of view. Branching off from Keynes were the national accounts, starting with Stone's and Meade's *National Income and Expenditure* (1944) and culminating, after four painful revisions, with the 1993 SNA, the binding rules for measuring economic value all over the world.

This development of value theory is indicated by the perpendicular arrows in Figure 6.1. The classical authors naturally spoke about the theory of value, having discovered, and been stunned by, the phenomenon of value circulation. They set the water and diamond riddle, which the marginalists then claimed to have resolved by means of mathematics. General equilibrium theory perfected the marginal approach as far as the topic of value was concerned, leaving nothing more to be explained. Consequently the succeeding generations of researchers turned to other fields of application of the theory. Becker's *A Treatise on the Family* (1981) was a conspicuous example.

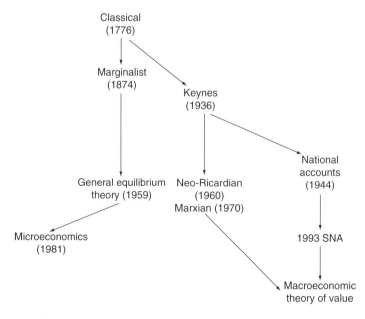

Figure 6.1   The evolution of value theory

By conquering other fields of science, microeconomic theory gained much, but it left much behind. It gained power due to the explanatory force of its abstract reasoning, similar to logic. But it gave up a concept that is typical of economics and found only there, the concept of a circular flow of value between production and consumption, created by the division of labour. It is a law of logic that when the terms of reasoning are made more general, something specific is lost, and this is what happened here, even if this did not involve a conscious choice.

Keynes himself employed only a rudimentary concept of value theory, being more concerned with the disequilibrium of an economy than its equilibrium. Sraffa considered equilibrium, but he was less interested in how it was arrived at in one market, than in how it worked between markets, the product and the factor markets in particular. He also addressed the question that had tormented Ricardo until his death: what should be the absolute standard of value? Bródy (1970) showed how Marx's theory of two sets of values – production prices and labour values – fitted into the same mathematical framework, adding this school of thought to the debate. However the debate remained purely theoretical and stopped short of statistical operations. The arrows on the lower right-hand side of Figure 6.1 indicate the thesis pursued in this book: that national accountants silently took over the development of the theory of economic value, and that the abstract ideas nourished by neo-Ricardians and other non-conformist schools are akin to it.

But the national accounts, one might object, are a statistical and not a theoretical device. How can they generate a theory? Having established our historical perspective, therefore, let us turn to a systematic definition of the theory of value. In very simple terms we can say that value theory is a theory that explains the following equation:

$$v = p \cdot q \tag{6.1}$$

where v is the value of a transaction, p is a concept of price, and q is a concept of quantity with regard to a commodity. The equation is well suited to illustrate both the difference between the microeconomic and the macro-economic approaches to value theory, and the fact that the national accounts are akin to the latter.

The difference between the two theories concerns the concepts and the relationships used in the equation. In the microeconomic approach, q stands for the quantity of a commodity expressed in physical units. To make these meaningful, not adding apples to pears, they must be homogeneous in quality. We may attach to the concept of homogeneity the idea that one can trade any particular item in the group with any other without affecting cost or utility (the 'fungibility' of a commodity in civic law). An equilibrated plan of production and consumption is derived from information on the technology, preferences and factor endowments of the economic agents. This plan includes a vector of appropriate prices as dual variables of the problem, which are equal to the marginal transformation rates between the commodities of each producer and to the marginal substitution rates of each consumer. As a result the value, v, of the transaction is determined by a product of price p and quantity q.

Not so in the national accounts! To begin with the order of deduction is reversed. Observation starts with the transaction value, v, this being the sum of an uncounted number of individual transactions within a commodity group. From this it follows that the commodity group is heterogeneous in respect of the quality of the commodities it contains. In general, one cannot replace an item with another (arbitrary) one without recontracting the transaction. Yet one item out of the many commodities in the group is picked and its price is taken as representing all prices in the group, regardless of how these actually move (see Chapter 5). The ratio of the overall transaction value, v, and the price of the representative commodity, p_i, is then formed to yield what is called 'volume', precisely in order to avoid any connotation of homogeneity that might be associated with the word quantity (SNA, 1993, para. 16.12). Volume always includes the quantity and quality of a good, blended indistinguishably together into an economic alloy. Thus we replace Equation 6.1 with

$$q = v/p \tag{6.2}$$

indicating the distinction both in terms of logical relationship and in terms of the content of the employed variables.

In this small example we use a method of presenting the national accounts that will be followed throughout the remainder of the book. The fact that we have contrasted Equations (6.2) and (6.1) might give the impression that only the first is applied to the national accounts, and not the second. This is not so. For the agricultural sector, for example, it is common to rely on Equation 6.1 to compile sales so that values are derived from quantities, and this in a quite sophisticated way. Satellite observation is used to estimate the expected and actual yields of cultivated fields, supplying data on well-defined, homogeneous crops based on market norms issued by the administration. Since all the observed production will be sold at equally well administered prices these are also known within a small margin of error, so that the transaction value can be approximated quite well for the national accounts. However, although this method may be used extensively in one particular area, it is still an exception to the general rule that governs the national accounts: the transactor/transaction principle (see Chapter 2).

National accounts aggregates are typically compiled by way of Equation 6.2 and not 6.1, and when we speak of the national accounts as a theoretical system we look at what is done typically, 'naturally' as Adam Smith would say, and we ignore the exceptions. We know, of course, that any logical system, when applied to practice, has to allow some room for exceptions. But these are not useful to represent and demonstrate the intrinsic structure of the system. The brilliant shine of an intellectually stimulating exception to a logical system must not blind us to its grey and ordinary rules. Incidentally, agricultural products would be a favoured object to which to apply the microeconomic model and its concept of homogeneous commodity were not their prices determined by anything but a market mechanism.

Are then, to repeat the question, the national accounts sophisticated enough to support a theory of value? Compared with microeconomics the national accounts are quite young, having been born in the 1920s. The appearance of the 1993 SNA was a historical achievement that was equal in weight to the arrival of the microeconomic equilibrium model. The national accounts have become like a bible, the concepts and methods of observation having developed to the stage of routine and rigour where they are now deeply embodied in the bureaucratic organisation of the statistical system of nations, having been partially incorporated in law. During this process they obtained their own rationality, which has been adapted to the subject matter observed in an economy. Since they are the only means by which quantitative information about flows and stocks of value in an economy can be created, they are not only a fitting but also a necessary object of study for a theory of value.

In this chapter we use the findings of the previous chapters to develop a bird's eye view of the encountered value theoretic issues. We contrast the micro and the macro approaches to value theory by means of their fundamental propositions. This is the axiomatic method, and while for each of our propositions there may be a discussion about its precise wording, their joint set will be coherent and comprehensive enough to form a theory. Detailing and reasserting these propositions will be the task of the chapters that follow.

Axioms of the microeconomic theory of value

We refer to Debreu (1959) as our basic source as this book became the cornerstone of the microeconomic approach to value theory. But as our purpose is to prepare the ground for the contrasts to come we cannot simply copy his propositions. We use six axioms to describe the content of Debreu's theory.

- Proposition 6.M1: there is an *l*-dimensional space of *commodities*, where *l* is any given positive integer.

The space of commodities is what can be called the Newtonian aspect of Debreu's theory, even if the space is not Euclidian. But similar to the absolute mathematical space within which Newton placed the observation of moving bodies, Debreu thinks of quantities (q) of commodities as the coordinates situating an economy. The answer to the question 'Where is the economy?' is thus given by 'At point q', which implies, of course, that one knows where point 0 is. The space dimensions are absolute in that their scale of measurement lies outside the envisaged model. They are physical units, specific to each commodity (that is why the space is not Euclidian), chosen once and fixed for all times and regions *a priori* of any economic mechanism.

Proposition 6.M1 is simple, yet it contains a seam of trouble when imposed upon the measurement of a market economy. For markets mean competition, dynamics, innovation and, in particular, new products, new ways of presenting them to the public and the death of old ones. The product cycle is the first thing a student of economic behaviour learns about as a mechanism to be aware of, and to make use of to keep her or his business going. In economics the problem of substituting new products for old ones is generally considered a technical aspect of the consumer price index. Here we see that its roots lie in a misfit between theory and empirical observation and the representation of economic phenomena. A market economy encountering repeated shocks in respect of changes in the kind and number of commodities cannot easily be pictured as a sun with seven planets moving around it in eternal and unchanging continuity. The number l of commodities is not quantifiable in a market economy, it is not given.

The number of categories contained in a statistical commodity classification is quantifiable, of course. But this has little to do with the number of commodities existing in an economy – it depends more on the precision with which one wishes to describe the economy. If the Danes have more items in their commodity classification than the Germans, this means that they want to look at their economy in greater detail (and are willing to incur greater costs) than the Germans, not that they enjoy greater diversity in terms of commodity choice. Counting the number of items in a commodity classification is almost as meaningful a statement about the economy as counting the number of intervals marked on a slide rule to obtain information about distance.

But never mind the critique, let us ask what Debreu means by the word 'commodity'. He does not provide a definition. He does supply some examples, but these serve more to illustrate what he means by homogeneity – wheat of this or that type in Chicago today but not in New York tomorrow – than to define what a commodity is. At one point, and in passing, Debreu (1959, p. 51) writes about production as 'buying in order to sell'. This would imply the classical definition of a commodity, namely any good or service that sells.

If this interpretation of commodity is acceptable to Debreu, microeconomic theory has made a point of departing from it. Generalising the concept of preference to ever more areas, such as education, marriage and procreation, proved a successful way to win Nobel prizes after the economic equilibrium theory had been completed, and turned microeconomics into a useful tool in many other fields. Indeed if 'commodity' is taken to mean anything that is delivered from one agent of a system to another, housework produces commodities, the environment generates commodities, even marriage does. All these things have to do with utility: if utility were not maximal, agents would not do what they are doing. As this is the path that microeconomics has followed since Debreu it is no wonder that he was the last to publish a theory of value in the strict economic sense. We continue with:

- Proposition 6.M2: the role of an *agent* is to choose a complete plan of action, that is, to decide on the quantity of his or her input or output for each commodity. Thus agents are characterised by the description of their choices and by their choice criteria.

- Proposition 6.M3: an *economy* consists of $(m + n)$ agents, where m and n are any given positive integers of producers and consumers.

The number $(m + n)$ does exist. Countries set up and maintain, at no small cost, a register of production as the backbone of their economic statistics, from which they obtain the number m. And the number n of households, or of heads in a kingdom, is the oldest figure in statistical history. But this concreteness is not what Debreu has in mind. According to proposition 6.M3, any number of agents can form an economy – they can number two, 20 or even 20 million, as long as they act in the same commodity space. Consequently any subset of $(m + n)$ producers and consumers form an economy. Foreigners may be included as well, as long as they are 'positive integers'. Disregarding money and its legal range of validity, proposition 6.M3 leaves the economy practically undefined.

While this criticism can be averted by assuming some implicit definition of a national economy, two other points are more severe. One is that the proposition speaks of plans of action, not action itself. The problem is the degree to which such plans yield data that are statistically accessible; not in a planned economy of course, but in a private economy with built-in data protection. This is the problem of observation. The other point is about the impossibility of dealing with each agent separately (information often having been drawn from sampling and other indirect sources), and what happens to the model when agents are separated into subsets. This is the problem of aggregation. The first of these problems is usually solved by inferring agents' ideas about plans and expectations from past data. More attention has been paid to the aggregation problem. We will not elaborate on this here, but it is well known in economics that the problem of aggregation of individual production sets and preferences is unsolved.

- Proposition 6.M4: there are *m producers*, each of whom chooses a production plan. This is a specification of the quantities of all his or her inputs and outputs within the commodity space on the basis of his or her knowledge about technology. The producer considers prices as given and maximises the resulting profit.

Debreu points out, (it is one of the aesthetic pleasures of the book that he never omits these restrictive comments even after a laborious exposition) that the proposition does not cover external economies and diseconomies, increasing returns to scale and the behaviour of producers who do not consider prices as given when choosing their production; points that have formed the playing ground for critique of the theory and attempts at modification. We leave these aside because they are not relevant to our purpose here.

- Proposition 6.M5: there are *n consumers*, each of whom chooses a consumption plan. This is a specification of the consumers' inputs and outputs within the commodity space, depending on their wealth. The consumers consider prices as given and maximise their utility.

Consumers' only output is labour of various types. Again, Debreu recognises the limitation of this proposition in that it does not cover the case where consumption by consumers is interdependent. A theoretical comment is provoked by the proposition in that Debreu considers labour as output produced by consumers from their consumption, including a minimum restriction for reproduction. Labour is their only output, all capital goods being produced by producers. Now if one considers that all consumption is earned through labour, either directly (labour income) or indirectly by inheritance (property income), or by the person earlier in his or lifetime (social income), would this not necessarily make labour the primary and only primary factor? Does Debreu implicitly employ a labour theory of value? We shall return to this question later.

- Proposition 6.M6: the plans of producers and consumers are in *equilibrium* if the demand of all agents equals the total resources. There is a price system that makes producers and consumers choose their plans in such a way as to attain equilibrium.

Prices are shown to be the rates of substitution and transformation between the commodities of each agent in the economy. The uniqueness and stability of equilibrium are not studied in the text, and are furthermore of no concern to us here. Our task is to answer our queries about observation and aggregation. Regarding the former, how does one establish as a fact the idea that an economy is in equilibrium? Does equilibrium imply that changes in quantity and price over time are zero? Or does this only apply to prices (equilibrium growth)? If these changes are not zero, as is usually the case, how does one distinguish a change of variables due to a change in the exogenous parameters of the model (technology, utility, wealth), which we may call equilibrium change, from a change due to the disequilibrium of endogenous variables at constant parameters? Concerning aggregation, if two commodities are aggregated at their observed prices – one with excess demand, the other with excess supply – is the resulting zero excess demand a sign of equilibrium at the aggregate level? The same applies to the aggregation of consumers and producers. These questions are a natural consequence of the microeconomic foundation of the theory and the attempts to apply it to macroeconomic statistical phenomena.

Let us return to the Smithian cases presented in the Introduction and see how they fit into the Debreuian theory. First, it costs twice as much to kill a beaver as it does to kill a deer. Assuming constant returns to scale and no capital at that primitive stage of society, the case is covered by the general equilibrium model, and if this is considered as an expression of the theory of labour value it must be accepted as a possibility within the general model. The water and diamond example is more interesting, concerning the paradox of value in use and value in exchange. How can a good with a high use value have a low value in exchange?

The marginalist school claimed to have solved the paradox by introducing the notion of marginal utility which now lies at the base of microeconomic reasoning. The argument runs as follows: Value in use is identified with the total utility that a quantity of a good provides to its consumer, and value in exchange with the marginal utility an additional quantity unit provides (Jevons, 1911, p. 78 ff). Total utility of a good is supposed to increase with the quantity of the good consumed while its marginal utility decreases. Thus diamonds have a high price, because they are few, so that the marginal utility of an additional quantity unit is high, although the total utility of all diamonds is low. In contrast, the total utility of the existing stock of water is high, it is essential for life, but its price is low, because an additional unit of it brings little additional marginal utility. The flaw in this argument has been mentioned in the Introduction (Chapter 1). The quantity units that are compared in this thought experiment remain undefined. What precisely is a lot of water as compared to a few diamonds? It may be that the inventors of this argument naively took weight as the common dimension, comparing a gram of water with a gram of diamonds. But this is arbitrary, just as any other choice of quantity units would be. Prices between different goods depend on the quantity units to which they are related, and since these are theoretically undefined, prices between different goods cannot be compared. The commodity space is not homogenous in its dimensions, and therefore the marginalists did not solve the water – diamond conundrum.

Axioms of the macroeconomic theory of value

In reiterating the microeconomic theory of value we did not intend to present anything new. Its subject matter is well known and contained in standard economic texts. We have merely pointed out the issues that need to be debated in this theory, setting the stage for the macroeconomic theory of value. We present its axioms, which are in fact the axioms of the national accounts that were introduced and elaborated in previous chapters, classifying them under the letter N for national accounts or M for microeconomics. In presenting them we summarise the arguments of previous chapters.

- Proposition 6.N1: an *economy* is the set of value transactions between economic units in a currency area.

This is how Richard Stone (1951, p. 69) begins when he puts the national accounts into an axiomatic framework. As emphasised earlier (Chapter 2), the national accounts are based on the transactor/transaction principle, meaning that their elementary data are the transactions between the institutions of an economy. A transaction is, in short, a transfer of value from the debit account of one agent to the credit account of another (payables and receivables). It is carried out through, and valued in, a specific currency. As an exception, value can also be transacted in kind, but these are marginal cases. An economy is the whole of these transactions.

It is easy to see that applying this theoretical definition in practice causes difficulties, because here again the number of transactions is not known and is impossible to ascertain. Not even an individual enterprise knows this number. What is known is the set of these transactions, known as the 'turnover' or 'sales' of an institution. The SNA (1993) adopts a more concrete definition in saying that an economy is the set of economic agents – it uses the term 'institutions' – resident on a national territory. 'National' means that the territory is under the rule of a single institutional framework of civic law and political power. Part of this framework is the central bank.

Leaving aside these subtleties of definition, proposition 6.N1 shows a distinctive difference to its microeconomic counterpart proposition 6.M1. The whole is defined before its individual constituents. Whereas in the microeconomic set of axioms the number of agents is abstract and thus arbitrary – any number of agents interacting with one another can make up an 'economy' – the national accounts take the nation as their object of study. Their notion of value resides in national institutions and their complex tasks, the material expression of which is the national currency. The currency is more than a numéraire, a mere denominator of value. It is the carrier of value, the daily token of a central bank and a functioning national credit system. It stands at the beginning of a macroeconomic set of axioms.

- Proposition 6.N2: the *agents* of the economy are institutional units that hold and manage individual property. They are the payers for and receivers of transactions.

If the parallels in construction do not seem too artificial, the contrast to the corresponding microeconomic proposition (6.M2) could not be more pronounced. Agents do not choose plans, but engage in transacting property. They are not characterised by limits to their choice, but by the legal form of their organisation, such as private or public corporation, governmental organisation, private non-profit organisation, household and so on (see Chapters 3).

All this is by its very nature observable – the characteristics and corresponding figures are kept in the records of the institutions and are aggregated by simple summation. The common unit of measurement is already there: the currency. Also note that the number of agents is not arbitrary, as in the microeconomic approach, but specified by the definition of economy. It is implied in the first proposition.

- Proposition 6.N3: *production* is an activity by a natural person in an institutional unit that is carried out regularly and against pay.

This proposition was argued for in detail in Chapter 3. Here we shall study its implications. The holding and management of property, the realisation of value through the creation of pairs of mutual claims to and liabilities for property require that the holders of such property have the right to defend it. They must be capable of suing and being sued, they must be legal units. They are of two types: natural and, derived from them, juridical persons. Only the first can carry out an activity. Consequently, inasmuch as in an institutional unit production must be performed by actual people, the proposition is evident.

The activity must be carried out regularly. Regularity of occurrence is an important criterion applied to many items in the national accounts, simply because in a statistical context single incidents are uninteresting. Concerning production, for example, painting a single picture and perhaps even selling it is not counted as production because it is not registered in regular statistics. But if the painting is a continuous activity, accompanied by an earned income, this is an economic activity and is registered on the production account. The activity must be carried out against pay. Since the national accounts trace currency transactions, it follows that they can account only for activities directly connected to such transactions (wages, salaries, entrepreneurial withdrawals and so on), which is the case if the activities are

carried out within the framework of an institution and are normally remu-
nerated through monetary pay (Chapter 3).

The macroeconomic definition of production (6.N3) is not dependent on
any concept of commodities. They do not exist at this stage of axiomatic
build-up. Instead we have a 'kind-of-activity' space, as laid down in the
International Classification of Industrial Activities (ISIC), for example,
where the product in question plays a role but is not the object of classification. Also, definition 6.N3 allows for more than one production purpose, not
only profit maximisation (called market production in the national
accounts), but various kinds of non-market production as well – provided,
of course, that this is performed in institutions, such as governmental institutions, private non-profit institutions and the like. This paves the way for
the inclusion of such institutions (forming a necessary element of a market
economy) in the system of national accounts in a natural way, and not by
way of an exception to the principles of the system. Having defined production we now come to:

- Proposition 6.N4: *products* are the output of production, delivered to
  individual units.

Products, rather than commodities, are the object of definition 6.N4, in
contrast to proposition 6.M1. The 1993 SNA deliberately made this alter-
ation to the terminology of its earlier versions, which implies not only an
extension of the field of observation from market production to the non-
commodities of non-market production, but also a restriction in other
respects. The field of investigation of national accounts is wider than that
of microeconomics. Figure 6.2 illustrates this schematically.

In microeconomic value theory the realm of property and the realm of
nature coincide. All goods and services are marketed and sold (that is, they
are commodities), and all commodities are produced. Also, in terms of
sectoring, a production unit is always identical to an institutional unit.
The exclusion of non-market production and non-product markets results
in the identification of property and production. This cannot be so for the
national accounts. However difficult the problem of duality appears and by
what provisional means it is solved in each national system, the existence of
the duality of property and production is never negated (see Chapters 2
and 3). Thus we have property items, which do not count as a result of
production (land, antiques, second-hand goods), and we also have production that is not brought to the market as property (non-market production).
It therefore makes sense, to distinguish between commodities, that is,
goods and possibly services that are produced for the market, and
other goods and services. The national accounts make a distinction
between commodities and products, and they account for the latter. Microeconomic theory does not acknowledge the difference, thus its field of

			Field of **National Accounts**	
			Field of **Microeconomics**	
			Flow accounts	Reconciliation accounts
			Produced assets	Non-produced assets
Field of **National accounts**	Field of **Microeconomics**	Market production	Commodities products	Commodities
		Non-market production	Products	-

Figure 6.2   Fields of investigation in microeconomics and in the national accounts

investigation is more restricted and less differentiated than that of the national accounts.

Financial assets, claims and money, in particular, are typical examples of non-produced commodities. Their value is not derived from production, but from exchange. On the other hand the value of non-market output is derived from production, from activities conducted by people in institutions and 'adding value' to the property of those institutions, and this irrespective of whether or not the output is marketed. The resulting output is called the product in proposition 6.N4. Non-produced commodities are not products, just as non-marketed products are not commodities. For both objects of value – commodities and products – it is essential that they are delivered to individual institutions or persons. Recognising the concept of individualisation and building it into the national accounts in a coherent and comprehensive way, was an innovation by the 1993 SNA in respect of the text of its predecessors and the result of a comparison with its late socialist sister, the Material Product System of Accounts.

This is an opportunity to look again at the concept of value in use, this time from a macroeconomic perspective. By means of the product classification, the transactions of an economy – which are mere amounts of money, and of abstract value in exchange – are assigned to certain categories of use. These specifications, still rather abstract, comprise a world of commodities but also describe a certain common purpose or meaning. 'Men's suits', for example, we may interpret as an expression of use value. A high use value relative to its exchange value would then mean that society values this product higher than the individual does. If a good is a merit good it may be subsidised (waterworks), and if it is a dismerit good it can be taxed (diamonds). As a collective good, and being of merit, it may even be provided at zero value in exchange and at public expense. Taking the argument one step further, one could interpret the difference between value in exchange – market price in the national accounts – and the cost actually incurred by the economy – value at factor cost – as a measure of the difference between value in use and value in exchange, one being the viewpoint of the whole, and the other being that of the individuals in a society. A microeconomic analogy to this double value concept is collective rationality on the one hand, and individual rationality on the other, as expressed in the cooperative and non-cooperative solutions to the prisoners' dilemma. Value in use may thus lie behind every argument in favour of government interference in the market, and if this is so, the concept has never been buried but has been with us all the time.

- Proposition 6.N5: *consumption* is the use of products that are not destined for production.

In the national accounts, this aggregate is called final consumption, in contrast to intermediate consumption, which is the use of products in production. Again we have a definition of activity, that is, something that takes time, in contrast to a plan, the making of which only requires a logical second. It would not be appropriate to put the definition in terms of agents, as in the microeconomic approach, because household production takes place in institutions of single entrepreneurship. Certainly the definition denies that labour is an output. All product classifications of the national accounts exclude labour. Whether consumption maximises utility is not relevant for the definition, but it is not excluded – we are free to believe that it does.

- Proposition 6.N6: the *value* of the currency is measured by the volume of consumption.

This proposition is tied to the first proposition (6.N1) in the same way as 6.M6 refers to its beginning, 6.M1. Please note that 'volume' is not the same as 'value', otherwise the system of axioms would be circular. 'Volume' is also not 'quantity' in the microeconomic sense. What it actually means is complex enough to warrant an extra chapter, which in our case was Chapter 4 on the index number problem. When the nominal value of a transaction, which is the value recorded in the circulating currency, is divided by the price index of private consumption it is called 'real value' of the aggregate. This does not mean that real values are 'true' or in any sense closer to reality than nominal values; on the contrary, nominal value is always the direct observation while real value is the result of an imputation within the accounting procedure. In practice one takes the consumer price index, the retail price index or the price index of private consumption, whatever its name and definition. All this has been explained in Chapters 4 and 5.

This completes the exposition of the plot of our drama, the protagonists having been introduced in a fair and equal way. Looking back at the two sets of propositions we find striking differences in content as well as in the systematic ordering of fundamental concepts, but also interesting correspondences. Figure 6.3 offers a summary review.

Our axiomatic presentation demonstrates the contrast between the two theories in great simplicity. The concepts of each theory are ordered by deriving the specific from the general in a natural way. Thus one can see the dominance of the commodity concept in the microeconomic approach, all other concepts being built up on it. In contrast, but in a similarly basic way, money stands at the head of the macroeconomic axioms, defining what can be observed as productive activity, and then as products.

The macroeconomic propositions lack a concept of equilibrium. Actually this is not altogether absent, but it is too complex to be included here and has been described in detail in Chapter 5 as a condition of price observation. The microeconomic analogue, 6.M6, could only be stated in such a blunt way because it is part of general economic knowledge. Its analysis and derivation are the substance of Debreu's book.

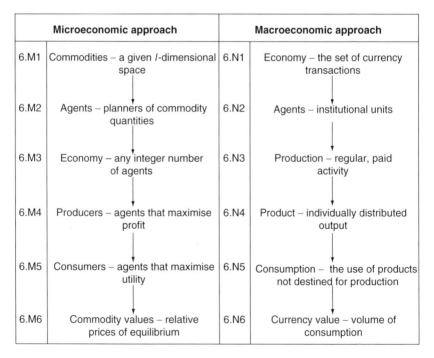

Microeconomic approach		Macroeconomic approach	
6.M1	Commodities – a given *l*-dimensional space	6.N1	Economy – the set of currency transactions
6.M2	Agents – planners of commodity quantities	6.N2	Agents – institutional units
6.M3	Economy – any integer number of agents	6.N3	Production – regular, paid activity
6.M4	Producers – agents that maximise profit	6.N4	Product – individually distributed output
6.M5	Consumers – agents that maximise utility	6.N5	Consumption – the use of products not destined for production
6.M6	Commodity values – relative prices of equilibrium	6.N6	Currency value – volume of consumption

Figure 6.3 Summary of the axioms of value theory

The contrasting of the axioms of the two value theories shows two things. Firstly, the axioms 6.N1–6 summarise a structure of the national accounts that is normally buried under piles of data problems and hardly visible in the daily workings of the accounts. Secondly, the contradiction between this structure and the concepts of traditional microeconomic theory is brought to light. In the following chapters the implications of this contradiction are spelled out.

7
Value Theory in the National Accounts

Having established a distinction between the two theories of value we return to the national accounts for further interpretation. The meaning of volume and price indices is investigated from a value theoretic perspective and the concept of real value is related to it in a systematic way. Finally, the old question of how to account for the use or possible misuse of nature is taken up again, and a new answer is given. It is stated that not just a particular part of GDP, but all of it must be attributed to nature as a gift from a factor that cannot be paid by any means.

The meaning of volume and price indices: explaining non-additivity

The principal axioms and concepts of national accounting practice having been established, this chapter considers the consequences implied by these axioms for the interpretation of the national accounts in terms of value. It is the most crucial chapter of the book in that it spells out the relationship between the measurement of economic value on the hand, and its theory on the other. It is doubtless the most difficult chapter, too. For besides liberating the process of price measurement from inappropriate theoretical claims, value theory must also lead to a positive interpretation of the procedures.

Two remarks about the history of the two fields of investigation will be recalled in order to defend this idea. First, the basic concepts of what is now called the microeconomic theory of value were developed before the national accounts. Microeconomic theory defeated the classical theory of value and formed the mainstream of economic thinking in the 1930s, when the national accounts had barely come into operation. Consequently the theory was not geared to problems of measurement. It was an architecture designed to mirror the impressive intellectual structures erected by the exact sciences of the time, but without apprehension of the material consistency of the bricks with which the edifice of empirical economic knowledge would later be constructed. Second, the very fact that this theory of value was constructed on a microeconomic base impeded its direct application to the national accounts, because these were essentially introduced to serve macroeconomic concerns. The microeconomic foundation of macroeconomics is a popular topic, but only in the sense that macroeconomic phenomena should be reducible to microeconomic theory, not the other way round. This one-way approach to research ignores the fact that individuals organise to form institutions, to share social values and to control individual behaviour. Since institutions are the units that create and report economic data, the national accounts have no option but to ignore this fact. Consequently their measurement of value includes the constraints of observation imposed by the economy's institutional framework. Value theory cannot be based on functional relationships alone (preferences and technology), it must incorporate the institutional framework as part of the value-generating process.

In what follows we raise some specific issues of the national accounts in order to demonstrate the change in perspective and understanding that takes place when they are identified as problems of the theory of value. We begin with an investigation of what can usefully be defined as equilibrium on a macroeconomic scale, which also opens up the possibility of determining its counterpart: disequilibrium. Concepts such as volume and price indices apparently have meaning only when there is a state of disequilibrium.

Having discussed the goods and services markets and their interrelationship, we turn to the factor market in order to investigate whether the national accounts, as a data-compiling framework based on institutions, are capable of measuring purely functional relationships, such as that between man and nature. Here it is appropriate to recall the motivating idea with which this interdisciplinary journey began, namely that the search for truth may turn out to be not so much successful as entertaining. It is envisaged that some of the conclusions drawn in this chapter will come to the reader as somewhat of a surprise and may or may not please her or him. In any event, the reader's ability to cease reading at any instant will incite us to be brief and clear.

As explained in the previous chapters, price statistics and national accounts use the formula

$$q = v/p \qquad (7.1)$$

dividing the price, p, of the representative commodity into the value, v, of sales compiled in a commodity group to derive the volume component of the included transactions. These being heterogeneous in quality the resulting number, q, is also heterogeneous and cannot be called a quantity, as in the microeconomic model. National accounting has decided to call it 'volume' in order to express the difference. Volume is the value of a transaction aggregate counted in terms of its specific representative commodity, at the elementary class level (Chapter 5). In this sense the resulting figure, q, allows a quantity-type interpretation. If an expenditure of 50 million euros is divided by 200 euros as the price of each piece of the representative commodity (for example a man's suit of medium quality and size) the resulting figure, $q = 250\,000$ [pieces], means that an expenditure worth $250\,000$ pieces of the representative commodity (suits of a particular kind) has been undertaken. In reality the price used in the operation is a composite index, such as the geometrical average of different local price observations, so that the homogeneity of the representative commodity is modified. Still, such an index contains sufficient quality characteristics to represent all the commodities in the group, and to distinguish them from all others outside the group at the same time. Each representative commodity is the standard of value in its class, and not of others.

This has an important consequence. Since a representative commodity is not a general standard of value, the volumes derived by means of the prices of different commodity standards are not additive. As each commodity group has its own specific representative, different volumes take on a different meaning, and thus cannot be directly compared. If the transactions volume of a class of tinned vegetables is measured in units of green peas, and that of men's suits in units of jackets, these volumes are naturally not additive because they are measured in different units. In this sense of non-additivity they resemble the quantities in microeconomic provenance. Non-additivity means that the figures have not yet been made homogeneous enough to be compared. In this way the characteristic that has been difficult to accept in the history of index number theory finds its justification in the analysis of the measurement operation of price statistics.

When, in an international comparison, experts have decided what item to use as representative of a commodity group between several countries, the volume $q = v/p$, derived from dividing the price of the representative item into each country's expenditure, is a multiple of quantities of the item. It is still a value measure, because the price differences of all other goods in the group are implicitly counted as quantities of the representative item, serving as the standard of value in the class. However these values cannot be meaningfully added between classes because they exist in different denominations, namely units of different price representatives. Similarly, when in a comparison over time the change in volume is distinguished from the change in price by means of identifying the latter with the price of the representative item, the resulting volume change is measured in physical units of the representative item. Again this precludes direct comparison between commodity groups. The expression

$$Q = \Sigma q \tag{7.2}$$

is not meaningful. To sharpen the distinction, let us relate the analysis to the concept of constant prices associated with the Laspeyres index. Volumes defined by means of the quantity Laspeyres index (Paasche for prices) are additive. But the interpretation is virtual. If the employed prices prevailed the volume would be as shown. This is a conditional statement rendered acceptable by a monopolist – a national statistical office that decides and authorises one and only one set of constant prices. As a thought experiment, imagine how the base dependency of growth rates and rates of inflation would be debated if the production of these figures lay in the hands of, say, politically competing agencies. The macroeconomic concept of volume can dispense with conditional statements. We have the information that an identical item that exists within the commodity group is capable of functioning as a value standard for the purpose of comparing value over limited time and space, and the interpretation of the resulting volume is in units of this standard of value. Value is measured in terms of the representative commodity instead of money, and is different for each class. There is no conditional statement involved.

Knowing that the range of validity of a particular value standard is restricted, we find a second heterogeneity. The standard commodity changes over time so that growth rates in different periods are not directly comparable, due to the heterogeneity of the standard of comparison. This will be better explained when we come to the equilibrium concept involved in this measurement. It stands in contrast to the constancy of the quality of goods implied by the Laspeyres index, of course.

Complementary to the notion of volume is the notion of 'pure price', which is usually defined only as a change in time. The pure price change of any commodity within a class is by definition equal to the price change of the representative item, the rest of the price change being imputed to quality change. Thus if the price of the representative item (a man's suit) rises by 10 per cent, this price rise is extrapolated to all the represented commodities, and if at the same time the actual price of some other suit in the class rises by 6 per cent, this means that its quality has decreased by 4 per cent, by implication of the measurement operation. Similarly, if in an international comparison the price difference is 2:1 of the representative item between two countries, and for some other commodity in the same class it is 3:1 the quality of the particular commodity is proportionately higher in one country than in the other. This is not only a necessary and meaningful interpretation, it also shows the limits of the measurement operation, which one must keep in mind in order not to overwork the technique. If product groups are very heterogeneous between times or between countries, the times and the countries themselves are incomparable, and no statistical technique can install comparability.

The relationship between volume, real value and value of money: measuring scarcity

If price and volume indices are compiled specifically for each product class on the basis of specific value standards, the question naturally arises of the possibility of a general price index based on a general value standard. This brings in the question of the value of money, which is the general value standard in a nation at a point in history. The value, also called purchasing power, of money is determined as the inverse of a general price level for all product groups. In accordance with our theory of relativity, such a general price level can only be constructed as an average of the different groups. The question is how to construct such an average. There are basically two positions. One is to take the consumer basket as the commodity standard, and this has been adopted by the world's central banks. The other is to base the purchasing power of money on GDP, as promoted by the international comparison projects. The positions are mutually exclusive in logic, and have not really been opposed to one another in practice, because neither thinks of the problem in terms of an integrated system of measurement of growth and inflation. The statistical reason speaking against GDP and in favour of the CPI is the fact that the first is not really a commodity basket. If determined by way of the expenditure approach it includes non-market products that have no price, and thus can hardly count in a standard for the means of payment. If determined by the product or income approach, it is a summing up of variables such as value added, which are partly defined as residuals and lack an intrinsic volume component or price representative that could be used in the price observation process. A volume may be imputed by means of statistical techniques such as double deflation. But it is not achievable by means of direct observation. The choice, however, is not central to our present argument.

By whatever commodity basket one determines the purchasing power of money, real product is the complement to purchasing power, that is, the nominal value of a transactions aggregate corrected for a change in the value of money. It is achieved simply by subtracting from all aggregates of the national accounts the change in price level. The method is called single deflation in the SNA (1993, para. 16.68) and is recommended there for mostly technical reasons. In our analysis it carries a distinct theoretical meaning, too. National accounts in real values are additive, and this reflects the fact that real values are still measured by means of a general value standard, in contrast to volumes, which are not. Real values account for the change in the measuring rod of value, all other relationships remaining the same.

Nominal value, real value and volume are three concepts of value that explain the flows through an economy. They are well defined for comparisons in space through the Geary–Khamis (or any other transitive) index system (see Chapter 4) and in time through the distinction between the specific and the general price deflator. The question is not whether 'volume' or 'real value' is the true concept of deflation, as some debates have it, but how to utilise them both in a mutually consistent way, each in their proper interpretation.

Thus we say that when the real value of a product group is lower than the volume, the specific price level is evidently higher than the average price level. Price is an indicator of scarcity. The distinction between the volume and real value of an aggregate allows us to measure scarcity on a macroeconomic scale. When the relative price is higher than the average price, this can be interpreted as a measure of greater scarcity. The price movements after the oil shock are an obvious example. When the price of a scarce good rises by 20 per cent, all others remaining constant, and the scarce good makes up 5 per cent of total expenditure, we find a general price increase of 1 per cent and a scarcity increase (relative price) of 19 per cent. We could also say that under ideal market conditions all prices would have dropped by 1 per cent and the price of the scarce good would have risen by 19 per cent, total nominal expenditure having remained constant.

Let us try to put these concepts into a systematic ordering (see chapter 4). Beginning with standard microeconomics, we have the value of an individual transaction, v, defined by a quantity, q, of a perfectly homogeneous commodity and a corresponding price, p, so that

$$v = p \times q$$

If, in contrast, we analyse the nominal value, V, of a macroeconomic aggregate of an unknown and innumerable number of transactions into a price component, P, and a quantity component, Q, statistical practice suggests the relationships shown in Figure 7.1.

The interpretation of the diagram is as follows. A pure quantity, q, is not meaningful for transactions aggregates. Even at the lowest level of the elementary product class there is already heterogeneity of products, made homogeneous by means of a common – yet specific to the class – value standard. The resulting quantity component contains both a change in quantity, q, and a change in quality, r, and is called 'volume', Q. On the price side there is also a decomposition. The concept of relative price, p, in the microeconomic sense is supplemented by a component of the purchasing power of money, pp. The relative price, p, stands for a measure of scarcity in the conventional microeconomic sense, while the value of money is a macroeconomic element of value. It is contained in every individual price and is called the 'pure price change' in price statistics of time and 'purchasing power parity' in international comparisons. Together they make up the absolute price level, P, and together with the volume component, Q, form the nominal value of a transaction aggregate, V. The nominal value is the bridge to the world of financial assets and transactions in the national accounts, because payments are financed by means of these operations.

Let us finish this section be reiterating the intrinsically institutional character of this analysis. Whatever is measured as volume, the price or the index

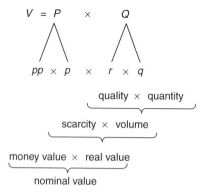

Figure 7.1   The relationship between macroeconomic value concepts

of real value depends on an underlying classification. The way in which observed transactions are grouped, the level of aggregation and the expenditure category assigned to a certain price representative are critical in this process. And again we must say that this shows the limits of useful national accounting. When there is no common classification between times or regions or sectors, comparisons are meaningless, if not virtually impossible. This is part of the inevitable relativity of value determination. Since value is determined within economies we can compare economies if they are different, but not too different.

Nature and GDP: the essence and appearance of economic processes

Every social tool has its own dynamics. When a new law comes into operation and proves successful in coping with social reality it looks as if the governing tool is adapted to, and passively mirrors, this reality. Later, when the tool has become standard, it assumes a life of its own and actually defines and generates reality. So it has been with the national accounts. Originally created to measure the wealth of nations, they now represent the *codex juris* of macroeconomic concepts, determining the content of any empirical analysis in the field. This must, at one time or another, be incorporated into the theory of economic value. As a necessary preliminary, a thorough understanding of the principles of national accounting is required, principles that must themselves be unravelled from the seducing diversity of issues that trouble the daily practice of measurement. One of the fundamental principles governing accounting is that of duality of processes and institutions (see Chapters 2 and 3). This is a principle of data observation that national (and business) accountants have developed on their own, unguided by economic theory. As a last step in the value theoretic interpretation of the national accounts, we build on this principle to address a topic that is popular for its simplicity but is nonetheless difficult to solve analytically (or at least the national accounting profession has struggled with it for quite some time): the relationship between economic variables and processes of nature.

As discussed earlier, duality is found in the two techniques of observation and imputation that are employed side by side in the accounts. It is embedded in the distinction between institutional units, which serve as the accessible basis for observation, and production or consumption units, which carry out these processes. Duality is inherent in the distinction between transactions of value, recorded in the accounts, and internal flows of value, imputed from the transactions in order to describe the physical transformation of values in production and consumption. Duality is captured by the principle of transactor/transaction and the principle of articulation, neither of which exists by itself. Without articulation – that is, the interpretation of observed transactions – these would be meaningless, one would see an unstructured flow of money. In the absence of observation the imputation of value would be arbitrary and void of empirical content. The combination of both describes reality. If we want to give this accounting principle a philosophical underpinning we may call it the combination of essence and appearance in economic measurement (Reich, 1989). The essence of economic value is production and consumption, because this is where goods and services originate and are destined for. However, under the division of labour these processes can neither be controlled nor observed directly. This can only happen when they have passed through a social mechanism of market evaluation, making them appear at the surface of observable reality. In this appearance they are unique, but whether behind them are 'labour values', 'production prices' or 'marginal rates of substitution', as different schools of value theory may claim, is a matter of imputation, of articulation of the data, to be inferred from the apparent phenomena. We have this paradox. The appearance of value is unique as a statistical measurement (the transaction), but the essence revealing the cause of value is not apparent and is open to economic debate. In this sense the microeconomic axioms presented in Chapter 6 cannot be proven wrong. What needs to be criticised is their claim for uniqueness, given the fact that the national accounts employ a different set of axioms, as explained in Chapter 6. The duality of accounting allows for different value theories.

The dual structure of essence and appearance in economic observation can be seen in the problem of determining value between the object and the means of measurement. Consider an economy that produces one good (corn) with one factor (labour). The two are exchanged so that a price can be established for the good in terms of the factor, and *vice versa*. If the first ratio falls, has the good become cheaper or the factor more expensive? Is corn the essence of the apparent value of labour, or is labour the essence of the apparent value of corn? This is what Ricardo called the 'invariable measure of value' problem, and failed to solve. Today, however, the Gordian knot has been cut, the role of Alexander having been assumed by our monetary authorities. They opted for corn – or in today's language, for the consumer basket of goods and services – as the measure of value, and a rise in wages against the consumer basket is defined as a rise in real wages, not as a lowering of consumer prices. This decision solved the practical but not the theoretical problem, because the standard is not invariable, set once and for all. It requires constant observation and adjustment, statistical maintenance so to speak, in order to be credible, and still it is invariable only in first-order approximation. It ties the standard of value to market observations of price representatives and expenditure classes of households. The 'invariable' standard of value is measured relative to this institution. This is an element of relativity in the concept of value that has found proper recognition in neither classical value theory nor its microeconomic descendent.

Another issue that reveals the duality of economic observation is the production boundary definition. Transactions as such can be grouped in many ways. If the national accounts use paid labour as essentially their criterion for the definition of the production boundary (Chapter 3), what does value theory say? For microeconomics the problem did not exist, as explained in Chapter 6. In the past, other concepts gained recognition at one time or another. Francois Quesnay's economic table was based on the notion that the boundary between production and consumption encircled the agricultural sector. Artisans were 'sterile', adding no value to their purchases. Interestingly enough the landlord class, which was generally agreed to be unproductive in those days, provided the proof of this production boundary because they lived on rent drawn from the agricultural sector. Rent as a non-labour income was seen as proof that the agricultural sector produced a surplus, and the generation of surplus was the indicator of productivity. Being not productive was considered a privilege, of course, and the exploitation of one class by another was not a social vice.

Marx, besides sharpening the distributional issue, showed how the locus of the payment of surplus value need not necessarily coincide with the locus of its generation in the product circuit. Labour values and production prices – or any other prices for that matter – diverge. Thus even if rent is paid solely by the agricultural sector, it may still have been generated as surplus value in the manufacturing sector and been passed on to the agricultural sector through the price mechanism. The generation of income and its distribution are separable in a money economy. Marx's analysis destroyed the prominence of the agricultural sector and set a new production boundary. Within the Marxian system this would be labour organised in a capitalist way, that is, all the labour that earns a profit. Socialist governments have interpreted Marx as drawing the line around the production of goods only, and constructed the material product system for their economies. In our view this approach is closer to Adam Smith's logic than the Marxian system, but we leave that to the experts.

In any case, if surplus is the criterion of productivity the Marxian definition is in line with that of Quesnay, except that he imputes surplus to industrial production as well. The criterion as such does not differ between the two authors. This is important in order to realise that the production boundary concept is not just a 'convention' and historically 'relative', but that there has been a logical development towards consistent and precise measurement. The later definitions have improved the earlier ones, with more insight into the economic process than before. Otherwise statements about the GDP structure of eighteenth-century France would be meaningless, each century having to be assessed through a specific definition of the time.

Today it is not the generation of non-labour income, of a surplus as the classicists say, but – on the contrary – the generation of labour income that determines the production boundary. Still this is a fully institutional delimitation of economic value, with all the difficulties expressed in well-known accounting paradoxes and discussed earlier (Chapter 3). It exists because it is in accordance with the conditions of statistical observation.

This brings us to our last point: the relationship between GDP, as an institutionally based value measurement, and nature, the actual haven of all economic resources. This relationship has given rise to considerable debate, and to the revision of the SNA in particular, but with the interesting result that after ten years of struggle not much has changed in this respect. Nature has still been left outside GDP. Can this be correct?

The original intention, prompted by ecologic concerns, was to subtract ecological damage from GDP and to derive an eco product in this way. However this would have increased the imputation part of accounting without a corresponding increase in observed data. We must recognise the fact that the depletion of nature is not measured in the concept of economic value in theory or in practice, and if the revised national accounts have decided to leave GDP free from environmental concerns this only reflects the fact that all the economic institutions that generate the value data for the accounts do likewise. It is also an indication that the concept of external cost, invented in the microeconomic context under conditions of *ceteris paribus*, is not adequate for dealing with environmental issues that are all-inclusive by nature. The national accounts have responded to the challenge by setting up accounts for non-value indicators, for example physical indicators of environmental states of affairs (SEEA, SESAME). Value theory might give a corresponding answer, not through the concept of external cost, which is a microeconomic concept, but by remembering its classical roots in a time when the intrinsic relationship between man and nature was more at the forefront of intellectual economists' minds than it is today. Let us look at a traditional and standard diagram in economics (Figure 7.2).

The standard interpretation of Figure 7.2 is as follows. The upper part of the figure illustrates the circuit of economic transactions, with money flowing from households (H) to enterprises (E) in payment for goods and services, and from enterprises to households in payment for factor services. The commodities bought for the money are shown in the lower part of the figure, the broken arrows indicating imputation rather than observation because the value of these flows in kind is imputed as being equal to the transaction value in money. Also imputed is the notion of an economic circuit between products and factors, both of which are measured by GDP. This is the dual structure of the accounts in all simplicity.

The first consequence of Figure 7.2 in respect of environmental accounting is obvious but ignored. GDP measures the value of output and the value of input at the same time. Saying that in accounting for GDP the national accounts only measure labour and capital, ignoring the input of nature, and that GDP is overvalued is therefore a one-sided view. GDP might just as well be undervalued, namely by the amount contributed by nature and not captured in the accounts, so that instead of writing off part of GDP for environmental use, that use should be added in order to reflect the value of all factors: labour, capital and nature. The subtraction theory holds only under the implicit premise that product markets determine the correct value of GDP, and not factor markets. But there is no reason why this should be so.

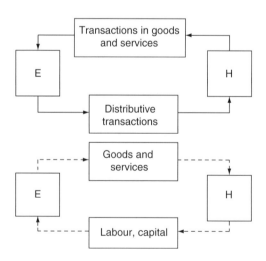

Figure 7.2 Circuit of economic flows

The correct argument, instead, is that the economic circuit is defined institutionally. It records transactions of property between people or their legal representatives. This is clear in the upper part of Figure 7.2, but it is also entailed in the lower part. Usually the lower part is interpreted not in terms of transactions but in terms of transformations. It is said that households consume the products and enterprises employ the capital and labour provided. But this is not the meaning of the figure, which is still situated in the field of exchange. Actually it shows the counterparts, the transactions in kind that follow the transactions in money in these business events. Thus it is still an institutional message. In fact all flows between enterprises and households are institutional by nature.

Consider Robinson Crusoe working all by himself, or any premarket economic organisation. In their work individuals produce for their own needs. Work is not paid but it is rewarded – just as much by the pleasure of its performance as by the eventual product. As all property resides in one pair of hands, there are no transactions and thus no values to be observed as norms of the division of labour. Producer and consumer are identical. Still there is a counterpart to human labour, and that is nature. Rather than taking the Robinson Crusoe economy as an illustration of the functions of capital, for which it serves rather poorly, we shall use it to demonstrate the intrinsic interrelationship between man and nature. Crusoe will not use a net for fishing in order to save time if that means depletion of the fish stock around his island and the necessity to build a larger boat to catch fish elsewhere, so that he eventually spends the same amount of time catching fish as he did before.

By using this parable in a different way and adding to it early physiocratic thought, it may help to explain GDP. Be it a one man economy, be it a highly developed division of labour, whatever methods a producer applies in his activity the result will be given to him by nature. There is no possibility of equivalence in this exchange – the sustainability of nature is not the same thing as the reproduction of capital. But it follows the rationale of the national accounts to say that GDP as a whole might be considered a gift of nature, measuring both the amount of human effort devoted to transforming nature to serve human needs, and the amount of nature acclaimed by man for this purpose. Not a particular part of GDP but its total measures what man has used from nature.

Theoretically, in physiocratic times land was the only productive source and only landlords collected a surplus. Marx's proposition that surplus can be generated anywhere and distributed through market prices opened the way to the macroeconomic view of the economic circuit of value. This was completed by the national accounts, where the notion of 'value added' to GDP as a total was implemented, reflecting the fact that within the division of labour all activity contributes to a common whole, a national product, a reward to labour from nature. A farmer, reaping his crops after tilling the land, will naturally consider his harvest in both ways: as a reward for labour and as a gift from nature. There is no reason why a complex economy should be different.

Thus Figure 7.2 might be complemented by a representation of an ecological circuit, operating in a third dimension – not one of transactions in money or transactions in kind, but of the transformation of matter, production and consumption (Figure 7.3). But there is no equality of flows in any kind of value. There is no division of labour between man and nature, no property shared between them, no economy installed.

This is the diagram found in the ecological literature of today. With systems such as SEEA and SESAME it became incorporated into the national accounts at large as a logical step after the recognition of the institutional character of the national accounts. What needs to be advanced is recognition that this also limits the concept of value in its range of application. Value regulates exchanges between people, and is only indirectly capable of controlling flows between man and nature. Again this follows less from microeconomic value theory than from its macroeconomic counterpart, where the institutional conditions of statistical measurement have been included in the analytical concepts employed. At any rate, if GDP in total is seen as measuring what nature has 'given' to a nation, then GDP is an eco product, a 'green' GDP that measures what a nation owes to its natural environment. Such a macroeconomic point of view is at least as plausible as the microeconomic view, adding up external effects of doubtful quantification.

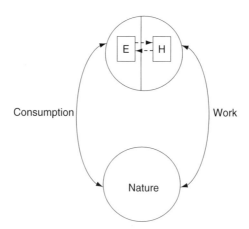

Figure 7.3   The ecological circuit of material flows

8
Value Theory in Economics

This chapter presents some conclusions from our analysis of the principles of the national accounts and the theory of value. The first section investigates the concepts of 'utility function' and 'production function', well known in the microeconomic realm. The second section deals with the concept of equilibrium, which needs to be refined beyond its microeconomic determination. The final section addresses what might be called a modern version of classical value theory, corroborating the claim that there are well-founded alternatives to the microeconomic analysis of value.

Functional analysis

The undefined function of utility

We begin with a formal issue. As the historical victory of microeconomic value theory was largely based on its being mathematical, opposition must also be phrased in that language, the language of purely functional relationships. Let us take a finding of the preceding chapters as the point of departure, namely that the division of a nominal aggregate value change into a volume and a price component is expressed in its mathematical (and ideal) form as a Divisia index:

$$\frac{dQ}{Q} = x_1 \frac{dq_1}{q_1} + x_2 \frac{dq_2}{q_2} + \ldots + x_n \frac{dq_n}{q_n} \qquad (8.1)$$

and

$$\frac{dP}{P} = x_1 \frac{dp_1}{p_1} + x_2 \frac{dp_2}{p_2} + \ldots + x_n \frac{dp_n}{p_n} \qquad (8.2)$$

where dq_i/q_i and dp_i/p_i are the relative changes (or logarithmic changes) in volume and price observed at the individual commodity group i, dQ/Q and

dP/P are the corresponding changes in the aggregate ($i = 1, \ldots, n$), and x_i are the weights of each commodity group i in the aggregate.

A short reminder of the underlying argument. The proposition is based on the axiom of temporal identity, which we revealed as being implied by statistical practice, coming to prominence whenever a case in doubt is being decided. The axiom says that when describing the state of an economy in a certain period of time only variables relating to this particular period should enter the accounts. In particular, growth rates and rates of inflation should be compiled as numbers that are independent of the choice of a base year outside the observed period, because such a choice introduces an element of arbitrariness and fiction into the observation. Therefore all the variables in Equations 8.1 and 8.2, the individual rates of change and their assigned weights, refer to the same point in time, this being the outstanding property of the Divisia index (see Chapter 4). The Divisia index is a differential defined at the limit of a time interval approaching zero. Such a mathematical ideal cannot be operationalised in practice. The chain index represents the proper approximation, with a Fisher formula as the element of the chain for each consecutive period.

It is known that differential functions exist for every well-behaved mathematical function, such as utility functions and production functions. Given any such function, the formula of its differential can be derived by means of standard rules of differentiation. The reverse is not necessarily true. Not every differential has a function to which it may be integrated. But interpretation of the Divisia index in terms of such a function requires integrability. Integrating given differential functions is like solving riddles because there are no standard algorithms leading to a result in all cases. The condition that a differential function must fulfil in order to be integrable to some other function is that the mixed differentials of second order are equal. The Divisia index does not fulfil this condition.

Traditionally, what is called economic index number theory works the other way round. It postulates a utility function and looks for indices that approximate it. What is called utility in this tradition may well be called value, for the purpose of comparison. If we consider the index as a differential of some unknown function of utility in its conventional form, we write

$$u = u(q_1, q_2, \ldots, q_n) \tag{8.3}$$

and the first differential is defined as

$$du = u_1 dq_1 + u_2 dq_2 + \ldots + u_n dq_n \tag{8.4}$$

where $u_1, u_2, \ldots, u_n$ are the first partial derivatives with respect to the goods $1, 2, \ldots, n$. This does not conform to Equation 8.2, where the relative changes have been addressed. It is more appropriate, therefore, to write the utility function in logarithms:

$$v = ln\ u = f(r_1, r_2, \ldots, r_n) \tag{8.5}$$

with

$$r_i = ln\ q_i \tag{8.6}$$

to which the first differential reads

$$\frac{du}{u} = f_1 \frac{dq_1}{q_1} + f_2 \frac{dq_2}{q_2} + \ldots + f_n \frac{dq_n}{q_n} \tag{8.7}$$

where $f_1, f_2, \ldots, f_n$ are the first order partial derivatives of the function f with respect to goods $1, 2, \ldots, n$. The function $f(r_1, r_2, \ldots)$ exists, given a certain vector of derivatives, if and only if the mixed second-order derivatives are equal. We must have

$$\frac{\partial f_{12}}{\partial r_1 \partial r_2} = \frac{\partial f_{21}}{\partial r_2 \partial r_1}$$

$$\tag{8.8}$$

Comparing Equations 8.1 and 8.7 we find that the equation

$$x_i = f_i \tag{8.9}$$

must hold if the Divisia index is to lead to a function of utility or welfare. The first order differentials of the suspected function must be equal to the observed weights of the index. In addition, due to Equation 8.8 we must have

$$\frac{\partial x_1}{\partial q_2} q_2 = \frac{\partial x_2}{\partial q_1} q_1 \tag{8.10}$$

as a restriction on the movement of the weights x_i. In reality, however, this restriction does not hold. On the contrary, the weights vary rather independently of the volumes of other commodities. As a consequence a unifying function that integrates the observed volume changes into a common function of utility, welfare or value does not exist. We must admit that on the macroeconomic level there is no function that assigns value u to a commodity bundle q_i. It cannot even be assumed, because any function would contradict the observed figures for the Divisia index, moving outside the realm of integrable functions.

Lack of integrability is tantamount to saying that the integral, if it is performed regardless, is path dependent. And the other way round: since the Divisia index is path dependent it follows that no aggregating function P or Q exists. We do not have absolute values.

Path dependency means that the value obtained for Q and P at time t depends on the values that variables p, q and x have assumed between times 0 and t on their path of change from one period to the next. It is not the concern of this book to argue whether such a quality is desirable for an index. All time series of price and volume data, if they are carried on long enough, finally fall prone to this characteristic. Instead of denying the fact it may be more fruitful to underpin it with some sense and meaning. The first step is negative, but necessary. We must dispense with the notion of an aggregator function for macroeconomic prices and quantities derived from their microeconomic counterparts. Aggregation changes the nature of these variables. P and Q are not what are called 'state variables' in mathematics, that is, variables that describe the state of an economy. What we do observe are not absolute values but changes in prices and volumes over time in a simple and unique way, described by the Divisia index. The question is whether one needs absolute values besides the observation of changes, which brings us to some wider considerations about equilibrium.

Before we move on, note that integrability would be achieved if the weights in Equations 8.1 and 8.2 were constant. The integrating function would be the Tornqvist index:

$$u = u_0 \, q_1^{x1} q_2^{x2} \ldots q_n^{xn} \tag{8.11}$$

This index would be independent of the choice of base year, except for a scaling factor. But even if the Tornqvist index were accepted as an ideal aggregating function it would not be additive between aggregates and would not correspond to the law of diminishing utility, one of the fundamentals of microeconomic value theory, so that the salvation gained for negating weight variability would be doubtful in terms of the theory's own goals.

One of the obvious and current contradictions between statistical practice and utility theory is the adherence to cardinal comparisons. An increase in the volume of GDP is measured in constant currency units, independent of diminishing marginal utility of increasing quantities of these goods.

Path dependency, or missing circularity, is a known characteristic of chain indices and thus as a problem of aggregation. But it is already implied at the elementary level of quality measurement in each product group. As the cotton/nylon-shirt example in Chapter 5 demonstrated, the quality difference built into time series of prices and volumes depends on the time and circumstance under which item substitution is effected. Circularity is missing in the same way as at the aggregate level of indices, only that here it cannot be concealed by means of a so-called constant weight index. Every price observation demands a judgement about quality, this being made under current circumstances, the only circumstances that exist at the moment of observation. The famous 'if' question of what might be if some other conditions of the past prevailed is not asked at the elementary class level. In this sense the Laspeyres index has always nourished an illusion that was not met by the elementary data collection process. More generally the technique of representing the prices of a group of commodities by means of one item chosen on purpose is not compatible with a theory of individually different and yet constant preferences. This is corroborated by the recommendation of modern index number theory of a superlative index in that the main advantage of this index over its predecessors lies in the independence of any specific preference function up to the second order. This recommendation pays witness to the diminishing relevance of such functions for the concept of price in macroeconomics.

The misdefined function of production

Microeconomic theory depends on the existence of two types of function: utility and technology (propositions 6.M3 and 6.M4 in Chapter 6). Having dealt with the first, we turn to labour and capital, these being the traditional independent factors (inputs) of a production function, of which GDP is the dependent variable (output). Let us study the Cobb–Douglas function as an example, stating a functional relationship between gross domestic product, Y, labour input, L, and capital input, K, in the following form:

$$Y = Y_0 \, K^\alpha L^{1-\alpha} \qquad (8.12)$$

The attractiveness of the function lies in its capacity to combine production with distribution, as expressed by the parameter α. The link to distribution is established by the assumption that the remuneration of factors is determined by their marginal productivities, so that

$$r = \frac{\partial Y}{\partial K} \qquad (8.13)$$

is the interest rate on capital, and

$$w = \frac{\partial Y}{\partial L} \qquad (8.14)$$

is the wage rate. Combining the three equations yields

$$\alpha Y = rK \qquad (8.15)$$

and

$$(1 - \alpha)Y = wL \tag{8.16}$$

The remuneration of the two factors precisely equals their share in income, and these add up to total income:

$$rK + wL = Y \tag{8.17}$$

Mathematically, this is a consequence of the linear homogeneity of the production function. Theoretically it establishes a link to microtheory, and thus an explanation of the mathematical phenomenon. This is standard textbook economics. A problem arises when one turns to the national accounts in order to apply the function to empirical observation. At that point one has to decide between nominal variables, real variables or possibly volumes. One may even think of physical quantities – the microeconomic concept. Textbooks are not explicit on these differences but they do matter, as we now show.

Beginning with nominal variables, the production function obviously holds. The national accounts furnish a nominal GDP, divided into two shares: αY for capital income and $(1 - \alpha) Y$ for labour income. They also furnish a nominal variable for aggregate capital, K, and a figure for total hours worked, L. By dividing each of these into their respective income shares one obtains a number for the profit rate, r, and the wage rate, w, both in nominal terms. The production function is fully determined.

Nominal values, however, are not what counts in a production function as they can be raised by effects other than those of production. Eliminating the effects of price changes, one looks for a production function in volumes or in real values. It must be admitted that the distinction between the two concepts in the national accounts is not usually considered in textbooks on production theory. For deflating nominal values one adopts the simple procedure of employing a general deflator, dividing each nominal variable by the general price index. This leads to real values, in the terminology of the SNA. It is assumed that the transformation does not affect the existence of a production function, but a little analysis shows otherwise.

Real values are defined as nominal values corrected for the change in the purchasing power of money given by the general price level, P, in the national accounts:

$$Y_r = \frac{Y}{P} \tag{8.18}$$

$$K_r = \frac{K}{P} \tag{8.19}$$

$$w_r = \frac{w}{P} \tag{8.20}$$

$$r_r = r - \frac{dP}{P} \tag{8.21}$$

Equations 8.18–20 define real GDP, real capital stock and the real wage rate respectively. The real rate of interest is usually defined by way of Equation 8.21, where the expression dP/P stands for the rate of inflation. Traditionally the production function is written in real variables. Thus instead of Equation 8.12 we postulate

$$Y_r = Y_0 K_r^\alpha L^{1-\alpha} \tag{8.22}$$

where the nominal values of GDP and capital stock have been substituted by their real values. If we do so by employing Equations 8.18–21 we obtain

$$\frac{Y}{P} = Y_0 \left(\frac{K}{P}\right)^\alpha L^{1-\alpha} \tag{8.23}$$

Equation 8.23 is different from Equation 8.12. As a consequence given a certain P unequal to 1, only one of these two production functions can hold.

The question is whether the equation in real terms is compatible with the accounting identities that hold in national accounts and are defined in nominal terms. Writing the accounting identity 8.17 in real terms yields

$$\frac{w}{P} L + (r - \frac{dP}{P}) \frac{K}{P} \neq \frac{Y}{P}. \tag{8.24}$$

This means that the accounting identity is not preserved in the transformation to real variables.

National accounts are compiled in nominal values. Additive consistency is preserved if they are converted to real values by means of a general price deflator. The nominal wage rate then changes automatically to the real wage rate, but the nominal rate of interest does not. In the national accounts the depreciation of financial capital through inflation is not part of the flow accounts at all, but is registered in the revaluation accounts, and that is where it belongs because there all capital losses and gains are treated together and consistently. In conclusion, inasmuch as the production function describes a relationship between factors of production entering into GDP, the nominal rate of interest is the appropriate indicator of capital income. Thus when speaking of factor rewards one must compare the real wage rate with the nominal rate of interest if national accounting identities are to be preserved.

Another point worth mentioning is that the famous conditions of marginal productivity can be obtained as a trivial result of accounting identities with whatever production function implies them. If gross domestic product, Y, is divided into any two factor incomes:

$$Y = rK + wL \tag{8.25}$$

it follows that

$$r = \frac{\partial Y}{\partial K} \tag{8.26}$$

and

$$w = \frac{\partial Y}{\partial L} \tag{8.27}$$

There is no need to prove these identities by recourse to some microeconomic assumption or function. They derive directly from the production function (8.25) of the national accounts, equating national product and national income shares.

And this is the only production function that really holds in the national accounts. Imagine any subdivision of the national economy by branch, region or otherwise. If accounting consistency is to hold between the labour, the capital stock and the value added of each subunit, the linear combination of factors is the only admissible function. The production function of the national accounts, – that is, the mathematical relationship between factor contributions and factor income – is linear by construction of the national accounts.

Conceptual analysis

Equilibrium in product markets

'Differences in prices at the same moment of time must be taken as *prima facie* evidence that the goods or services concerned represent different qualities of the same general kind of good or service' (SNA, 1993, para. 16.110). If we take the preceding statement as a definition of the relationship between quality and price, deduced from the rules of statistical practice (Chapter 5) the question arises of how to introduce this insight into the theoretical market model that embellishes our economics textbooks. Projecting this statement onto economic theory, it follows that the so-called 'pure price change', measured with identical products, which is what price statistics strive for, aims at the value not of the commodity but of the numéraire given in exchange. The devaluation of the numéraire does not show in a standard market diagram of relative prices versus quantities with an arbitrary numéraire. But considering the quality of the price representative constant over a short time means that for this particular time interval the supply and demand of the commodity being observed are considered not to have changed. Its market being in equilibrium, the commodity serves as the momentary store of value against which to measure the purchasing power of the means of transaction. Consequently if there is a price change in spite of constant commodity conditions, this must be a purely monetary phenomenon. The pure price change relates to the observation of a pure purchasing power change in respect of money. This is the logic of working with product items that are postulated to be identical in all economic aspects. It puts into operation a notion of inflation that 'involves the general level of prices as compared to relative price adjustments which reflect changes in market demand and supply conditions bearing on specific goods or services, such as oranges, ladies' footwear or gasoline' (Diewert and Montmarquette, 1982, p. 22).

In essence then, our analysis of price observation practice on the one hand, and microeconomic theory on the other, shows that what is called price, or value, in theory is called quality in price statistics. In other words, when price statisticians say that two products are different in economic quality they mean commodity value, as established between the forces of supply and demand. And what is called a pure price change in statistics is conceived as a change of numéraire in theory. It signifies a change in the purchasing power of the means of payment – in the value of money. These changes differ in different markets, but they have in common that they are not due to the observed product. Under conditions of perfect liquidity between markets the change in money value will be the same in all markets. Empirically the average is the approximation of this equilibrium, so that even if the price statistician estimates a pure price change for an identical item, this includes the disequilibrium or scarcity component *vis-à-vis* the other markets and can be adjusted only after all price observations have been made and the general price level has been determined.

Contrary to what is commonly supposed and although the same words are used, 'price' in theory and pure 'price' change in practice are not the same concept. The price considered in a microeconomic market model is a relative price in terms of other goods. The numéraire is irrelevant and cancelled out. This is not the case with price observation in statistics. Here it is not the relative but the absolute price change that is sought, and the condition of item identity means that the demand and supply functions remain stable so that an observed price change can be attributed only to the monetary side of the market, as a change in purchasing power. Relative movements can be derived from the data, of course, but they are secondary. Since the concept of a pure price change is defined as a value change that has not been caused by a quality change – that is, a change in the conditions of supply and demand determining the commodity conditions of the market – a price change, if it occurs, can only be due to a monetary influence. In this sense the measurement of inflation is inherent in every price observation even when this may not be directly recognised. The different price level changes for different commodity groups show how different markets react to the monetary change that is captured by the measurement, the overall rate of change of purchasing power being defined as their average.

If this interpretation of statistical practice is accepted and we set out to draw a conventional demand–supply diagram for the representative commodity, there is not really much to draw. The observed price change is part of the numéraire by definition, and thus invisible in the diagram, and the quantity, q, of the commodity being sold is not known and probably unobservable. Remember that for the price representative perfect homogeneity is assumed, which includes institutional characteristics such as points and conditions of sale. The quantity of goods falling under these specifications is impossible to define in any empirically meaningful way. We have a condition of complementarity here. The more homogeneously we define a good, and thus the more precisely we define a price, the less exactly we estimate the corresponding quantity of the good.

If forces of demand and supply are deliberately excluded from the observation of price representatives we may be more successful in studying them at the level of the elementary class, because here the duality of a price and a value component is realised statistically. However the specific meaning attached to these components through the measurement process must be taken into account. For reasons of simplicity, let us assume that each elementary class of the statistical product classification coincides with a market. The price change in this market is given by the price change for the corresponding price representatives, aggregated to a specific elementary index. The quantity component is derived by applying the index to the nominal value of the aggregate. As the price change is only attributable to the means of payment, we have no observation of market forces. The volume change includes both changes in quantities and changes in the quality of the products, included in the class. In other words volume and real value coincide at the elementary aggregate level.

As stated before, the measurement of volume change in a product class can be interpreted as a measurement in terms of the representative commodity. Volume is expressed as a number of quantity units of this commodity, derived by dividing the price of the representative commodity into the value of the market turnover. So by definition there are no forces of supply and demand in this price and volume change. These forces cannot be observed in the national accounts. As was discussed in Chapter 5 the national accounts are based on the a priori assumption that markets function properly. Prices that are observed on imperfect markets under lack of information, discrimination or limitation of choice are not acceptable as value measurements. Consequently, what the price indices of the national accounts show is not equilibrium within, but equilibrium or rather disequilibrium between markets.

In Chapters 4 and 5 path dependency was shown to be an intrinsic feature of price and volume indices. Although its lack of circularity is a serious argument against the Divisia index at first sight, when gathering the arguments from the different fields of empirical investigation we found that temporal identity of the variables entering into an index number (Chapter 4) is deeply engrained in all of these measurement operations, so that even a Laspeyres index does not really do away with it. Mathematically, temporal identity is a cause of path dependency. But it is more than that. In terms of economics, it expresses the fact that the compiled figures are disequilibrium rather than equilibrium variables.

Our investigation of the statistical treatment of quality change has substantiated the hypothesis that the national accounts work differently from, or are even the reverse of, microeconomics. Instead of postulating homogeneity for a flow of commodities, allowing for diversity by means of a large, potentially infinite number of such homogeneous goods, the national accounts are bound to work with a finite number of commodity groups (some thousand), where heterogeneity in time, space and selling conditions is recognised as a normal state of affairs and is handled by means of price representatives. This heterogeneity is so characteristic that the price dimension (money unit/physical unit) may not be the same even within a single commodity group. Consequently the notion of price in the microeconomic (and everyday) sense is replaced by that of a price index, where the absolute level is arbitrary and only its change is a statistical datum.

Working with rates of change instead of accumulated index levels is in line with the path dependency of these indices. To illustrate this by way of an everyday example, when speaking about the average height or average weight of a population one never mentions the overall height or weight, although the sum of the weights or heights of all members is calculated in order to arrive at the average. In the same way, average growth rates or rates of price change can be formed over several years, of course, but their accumulation to levels is meaningless. We can never, under the conditions of valid national accounts, return to the production attained in some earlier period of history, nor can we jump into a technology of the future. Each time has its own system of prices and volumes and this is expressed by path dependency.

Ignoring absolute price and volume levels also corresponds to intuitive understanding. As we have pointed out repeatedly, the prices of different commodities cannot be compared. To say that diamonds are more expensive than coal or deer are more expensive than beavers is nonsense unless one arbitrarily fixes certain quantities of these goods. But these are variables in dynamic markets. In dynamics we have velocities. In this sense what can be compared are price differences and volume differences per unit of time not their absolute figures. In mathematical terms, price and volume indices are not state variables of an economy.

Equilibrium and disequilibrium between product markets

The equilibrium addressed in the conventional market diagram of supply and demand cannot be observed in the national accounts. Equilibrium in a market was attained before the values were measured in the national accounts, so these changes do not reflect the working of supply and demand in markets at given demand and supply functions, but rather the movement of market equilibria, the combined movement of these functions. Remember that the meaning of the price index is a pure price change in the sense of a monetary phenomenon. Generally this pure price change is different in different markets. This happens because the linkages between markets are imperfect, when income and finance do not flow freely between them and there are barriers to overcome. Then we have disequilibrium between markets, and this is what the relative price changes show. Market barriers have prevented the flow of resources to equilibrate all the product markets between each other in the economy. Separating the different components of disequilibrium we have

$$\frac{dV_i}{V_i} = \frac{dp_i}{p_i} + \alpha + \frac{dq_i}{q_i} + \beta \tag{8.28}$$

The nominal change in the transactions aggregate of a market, dV_i/V_i, can be explained by a relative change in the price level compared with other markets, dp_i/p_i, by the overall rate of inflation, α, by the relative change in volume, dq_i/q_i, and by the overall real value increase, β. The sum of the last two variables is the increase in volume of a particular market:

$$\frac{dQ_i}{Q_i} = \frac{dq_i}{q_i} + \beta \tag{8.29}$$

and the sum of the first two is the increase in the specific price index:

$$\frac{dP_i}{P_i} = \frac{dp_i}{p_i} + \alpha \tag{8.30}$$

where α is the general inflation component. If deducted from nominal changes it gives rise to the notion of real value, as defined in this book in accordance with the SNA. The concept of real value accounts for the change in the measuring rod of value, money, as explained above. The equation

$$\frac{dp_i}{p_i} + \frac{dq_i}{q_i} = 0 \tag{8.31}$$

is of interest because it describes a special case. When relative price and volume changes are equal in size and of opposite sign in a market, the share of the market in overall expenditure does not grow. This has an interesting interpretation. Expenditure shares are an indication of how an economic unit spends its money. Private consumption expenditure of households is thus structured so as to maximise utility of every houshold, a well-known postulate from microeconomic theory. But whereas microeconomic theory tries in vain to derive an appropriate price and volume index for utility functions allowed to be of any kind except that they are mathematically well behaved, in the national accounts we can work the other way round. We can say that the expenditure shares of individual commodity groups within household expenditure express household utility or preferences in that the last dollar of each share must carry equal marginal utility. Consequently, a change of expenditure share in time indicates that preferences have changed between product groups while the expenditure structure remaining constant means that preferences have remained constant. Similarly in space where differing expenditure shares between nations mean that these differ in their preferences for commodity groups, and if expenditure shares are equal we have truly one world economy.

In the next step we may even infer a definite utility function from this interpretation. If constancy of preferences is identified with constancy of expenditure shares the utility function must be defined by these shares and is identical to the Tornqvist index (equation 4.17). This is a well-known result of economic index number theory, but in the context of national accounts it does not have much relevance beyond a mere analogy, because no additional information is gained by first constructing a national welfare function from the aggregate consumption expenditure of national accounts and then deriving this expenditure again from it.

Having interpreted the relative changes in prices and volumes in different, imperfectly interconnected markets we now look at the aggregates as a whole. For total private consumption expenditure there is no relative price change, because an increase in its price level is equivalent to the general price level and a purely monetary phenomenon, by definition. Consequently the aggregate demand function, popular in macroeconomic textbooks, is meaningless. Saying that aggregate consumption responds to price implies that the price, being relative by definition, should be compared with some other price. But this other price does not exist, because in this comparison it is always the consumption bundle that serves as the standard of value. Hence it has no price itself. If the aggregate demand price is divided by the price level one obtains 1, they are identical.

In a static system we observe nominal values at the macro level, all price indices standing at 100 by definition. Volume, real value and nominal value are the same. Separation into a price and a volume component is feasible only under dynamic conditions of change due to economic disequilibrium.

In space, too, differences in prices are observed only under conditions of disequilibrium. And the very concept of equilibrium depends on, and is relative to, the classification applied to it. There may be a zero price change in the aggregate, but two offsetting prices changes in the subaggregates. A proper classification requires a study of institutions in order to define the relevant markets. The national accounts do not render information about disequilibrium in markets. On the contrary they wait until equilibrium has been attained or restored, and then determine possible disequilibrium between markets. But what you call a market depends on the applied classification.

Before we turn to the final section let us take a brief look at the spatial dimension. Remembering the way in which and the implicit assumptions with which volumes and purchasing power parities are defined in the system of spatial price and volume, such as the Geary–Khamis indices, we can surmise that disequilibrium in space is expressed by similar indicators as those for time. We observe that the prices of world commodities differ in member countries. This contradicts the assumption of a world commodity, unless we again interpret it as a sign of disequilibrium in space, of barriers to communication between countries, destroying the homogeneity of the world market. On the basis of microeconomic theory one would interpret price differences as differences in taste. But that would not be sufficient. If the commodity in question is considered a true world market commodity it has to sell at the same price wherever it is offered, otherwise it would have to be considered a different commodity. We can carry the argument even further. Expenditure shares are different between countries. Inasmuch as these differences are statistically significant they indicate a disequilibrium, in the same way as a growing or shrinking market indicates disequilibrium in time. If the world were truly one market, productivity conditions would have equalised and become independent of regional variables, and income would be the same irrespective of where people live. This is an illusory condition, of course, and we are not saying that it would be a desirable state of affairs. Nor are we saying that equilibrium is desirable. All we are saying is that regional differences between markets indicate regional disequilibrium between them. And the difference between the world price and the country price is a sign of relative scarcity, as it occurs in temporal disequilibrium.

Links to the classical theory of value

Asymmetry of labour and capital

A significant example of asymmetry is pictured in Figure 8.1. The national accounts are based on two fundamental distinctions. The first is that there are units for production and units for consumption, and that in principle the two are distinct. Perhaps it is even better to think in terms of time budget surveys and say that human activity is divided into two separate sets of production and consumption. In either case, this is the distinction that allows us to call a certain flow of goods 'final', in the sense that it leaves production, and to equate it in value to a flow of income from production, called 'primary'.

The other fundamental distinction is that between labour and capital income. Figure 8.1 demonstrates an interesting structural difference between the two kinds of income in the national accounts. Labour income is paid from production units (establishments) to consumption units (households). Thus it is a distribution of primary income, of the value added generated in the unit employing the labour. Capital income is paid and received throughout the economy. In fact the major part of interest payments flows within the producing sectors, mostly between non-financial and financial institutions, but all these institutions pay and receive interest at the same time. This implies that interest flows must be interpreted as a means of distributing value added between the owners of capital, rather than as an indicator of where this value added has been created. Proof of this is the rule that the capital income earned by households does not indicate production there, and this is not a mere convention in the national accounts, but corresponds to economic common sense. No one receiving interest on their savings account would identify this income with the earnings of the 'economically active' people working in the bank. Nor would they believe that the value added out of which the interest is paid originated in the paying bank. They are more likely to trace it back to the producing sectors, but the precise place of origin cannot be determined.

Capital income, therefore, is secondary income in the sense that its original production source cannot be determined. It distributes income that has been created from economic activities, but not necessarily activities by the institution that pays it. In fact capital income of any amount can flow between production institutions without contributing to GDP, the flows being netted out within the sectors. Consequently saving, although it is

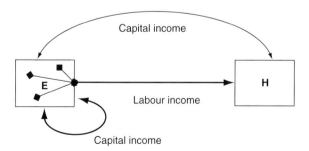

Figure 8.1   The flow asymmetry between capital income and labour income

rewarded by the bank, is not an economic activity, neither in time budget surveys nor in the International Standard Industrial Classification of Economic Activities (ISIC), nor in the national accounts and the macroeconomic theory of value.

A further indication of the asymmetry of factors comes from the observation that in the national accounts all labour income is counted as gross. In other words, wherever a dollar of labour income arises it is counted in GDP, and its source is counted as an economic activity even if it occurs without profit (non-market activities). Labour income is never netted out against another labour income. In terms of circuit theory these flows are parallel, each adding their specific value added to the total result of the division of labour. Not so for capital income. Enterprises and government agencies have large payments, but also considerable earnings in interest and other capital income. The gross amount of these earnings is not shown in the national accounts, but netted out within sectors. This reflects the fact that capital income is part of finance rather than production, and these flows are not parallel but sequential. In fact the full amount of interest paid on capital by an economy is usually not considered as a significant variable in economics. This is natural and common sense. But it also proves that capital income distributes, rather than indicates, value added.

The mere ordering of transactions expresses this asymmetry. Formally, value added is determined in the production account, before interest payments have been made or received. Thus value added describes the result of each production process at its source. Labour income is not received by production units, so it is entirely clear how much value added of each establishment has been distributed. Labour income is a valid indicator of the source of income at the observation level. Thus in some ways the national accounts treat labour as if it were the one and only primary factor of production.

This brings us to a historical digression. We have been taught that the labour theory of value is outdated. Some economists outside the mainstream tried for a while to keep it alive, but as it was claimed by socialist economics it was doomed to be discarded altogether when socialist economies failed. We do not want to revive the theory here, partly because the term 'labour value' is so poorly defined that one creates a lot of unnecessary controversy simply by employing the word. But if for our purposes we assume that 'labour' is what in the national accounts is called 'economic activity', a lot of propositions held by the classical theory of value can be rediscovered as theoretical elements of the national accounts. This begins with the distinction between primary and secondary income, and extends to the concept of value assigned to products. It will be entertaining to sketch the traits of the idea without going into it too deeply.

The distinction between value and price

The classical theory of value is characterised by three features: it considers economic value as an objective phenomenon, it assumes proportionality of value and quantity, and it is macroeconomic in nature, differing in all three aspects from its microeconomic sister. In the past the view of value as an objective as opposed to a subjective category was the focus of debate, as was the idea of marginalism, which gave the new theory a claim to scientific revolution in the nineteenth century, opposing the concept of value as an average characteristic. The contrast between the macroeconomic and micro-economic approaches to the value concept has not found a topical place in the history of economic thought, partly because it only became possible to identify the distinction after the national accounts came into being. Today it shows in the lack of, if not barriers to, communication between national accounting and theoretical economics, of which it is perhaps the cause. In classical writings the macroeconomic line of thought can be recognised in the concept of economic circuit, applied, for example, to the idea that all products can be 'dissolved' into labour.

In this section we describe the kinship between the national accounts and the classical theory of value in all three aspects, not with the intention of rejecting the microeconomic approach to value theory in general – that would be extreme – but of demonstrating its limitations, and thus revealing the necessity to enlarge our textbook theory of value for the purpose of understanding, and working properly with, figures taken from the national accounts.

The idea that value is an objective concept is evident in the search for an objective standard. In subjective value theory such a thing is not needed, because commodities are fully and directly compared among themselves without the intervention of a third object. The standard of value degenerates into a numéraire. One consequence of this is that the distinction between a numéraire and a standard of measurement has been neglected if not ignored in economic studies generally. This very question troubled Ricardo until his death, and one cannot reintroduce it in better words than his own (Ricardo, 1951): 'By exchangeable value is meant the power which a commodity has of commanding any given quantity of another commodity, without any refer-ence to its absolute value.' This first sentence of Ricardo's last work, entitled *Absolute Value and Exchangeable Value'*, contains the roots of the later histor-ical development. It defines prices as relative variables, an idea pursued by the microeconomic school. But it also refers to absolute value, a concept put aside by that school and only revived through macroeconomic necessity, although always confronted with opposition from the value theoretic side. The question of how to measure inflation has been imposed on economic theory by the necessities of life. A stern microeconomist would hold that there is no such thing as a general rate of inflation, but that there are millions of individual prices, the changes in which have their own explanation and must not be aggregated into a general change. The central banks of the world have put an end to this reproach in that they have made the general rate of inflation one of the crucial variables of economic policy, measured by the consumer price index. They know that there is an absolute standard of value, and are committed to keeping it invariable. Thus by means of monopoly and authority the central banks have resolved Ricardo's problem. Let us see in what way.

To Ricardo an 'absolute' standard is the same thing as a 'perfect' or an 'invariable' one. This creates a problem: 'There can be no unerring measure either of length, of weight, of time or of value unless there be some object in nature to which the standard itself can be referred and by which we are enabled to ascertain whether it preserves its character of invariability.' And the crucial answer: 'It has been said that . . . such a standard is to be found in the labour of men. . . . Of all the standards hitherto proposed this appears to be the best but it is far from being a perfect one.' This is the labour theory of value, although in its abstract presentation it allows for a typically Ricardian view.

In any case, central banks do not count labour time in order to arrive at their standard of value. In this sense the classical theory of value has definitely been rejected. Nevertheless central banks keep much more of an eye on wage rates than they do on profit rates for the purpose of guarding against inflation. Ricardo, on the other hand, deals with some astonishingly modern issues: 'By many Political Economists it is said that we have an absolute measure of value, not indeed in any one single commodity but in the mass of commodities.' Is this not the CPI? Ricardo continues:

> This measure might be an accurate one on many occasions, but suppose that on such a comparison I found that with respect to a great number gold had altered in value, and with respect to another large number it had not altered, but cloth had; how should I determine whether the cloth or gold had varied? . . . how should I know that the commodities to which I thus compared them had not themselves altered in value?
>
> (ibid.)

Ricardo did not know the techniques of establishing a consumer price index. Had he known, would he have accepted them?

To choose 'a mass of commodities' as a value standard, a commodity basket as we say today, seems fully acceptable to Ricardo in theory. His objection refers to the indeterminacy of the concept. There is, firstly, the question of which basket to establish. Today this is the private consumption basket, which is also questioned every once in a while. There is, secondly, the problem of relativity. If one commodity is compared to a mass of them, how does one know that it is this commodity that has changed and not the mass?

The answer to this question is contained in what we might call the law of gravity in the national accounts. In defining the rate of inflation as an average of price changes, one succeeds in separating a general influence from a particular condition. Since money is involved in all transactions, it is reasonable to identify the average change in prices with the monetary factors of value, and the relative changes with the specific conditions of each commodity. This convention holds even for the prime examples of absolute standards Ricardo refers to, namely length, weight and time.

Our investigation of the treatment of quality change in price statistics has supplied some tools that enable us to be more precise. The commodities chosen as the standard of value for their particular product group are called price representatives. They are chosen on the condition of being sold regularly and in large quantities at stable market conditions. This technique answers Ricardo's concern: 'How should I know that the commodities to which I thus compared them had not themselves altered in value?' Commodity experts know, and while the concern has certainly not disappeared, it has been transformed from a theoretical objection into a practical rule of measurement in the determination of value. Thus we can conclude that Ricardo might go along with the consumer price index, as it is prepared today.

Neo-Ricardians, following the lead of Sraffa, apply as the standard commodity a different commodity basket from the CPI, namely the dual vector to production prices. This takes us to the second trait of classical value theory: proportionality. Ricardo writes: 'Exchangeable value and proportional value mean the same thing.' In contrast the essence of the marginalist revolution consists in the thesis that exchangeable value is not proportional to quantity but decreasing. The proportionality rule is intrinsic to the national accounts. Pragmatic economic theory has done away with marginalism on the macroeconomic scale by introducing the following principle: if a large factory will produce less than that produced by two factories of half the size, the latter will be built and not the first. We can apply a similar principle to the demand side. Assuming each person buys at marginal utility, the price remains the same with proportionally increasing numbers of purchasers and producers. Turning to the national accounts proper, proportionality is even more visible. It is common sense that the accounts of a nation should be separable into linear subsets, such that the sum adds up to the total, and this regardless of how one divides the subsets. Accounts divided into the north and south of a country should add up to the total in the same way as accounts for the east and west. Linear separability implies that prices are the same in all subsets. As a result they are independent of quantities, in contradiction to the microeconomic model.

As noted in Chapter 6, the boundary of an economy is not defined in the Debreu model. In this model two individuals can form an economy just as easily as two million. But any economy of two million individuals can also be considered as a set of one million economies of size two. Under marginal conditions the resulting prices are not the same. Proportionality of value assures this aggregation rule, which is essential for macroeconomic studies. *Prices, Proportions and Planning* is the title of a book that puts this feature of the classical theory of value at its centre (Bródy, 1970), and we take it as a guide for elaborating on the proportionality of value in the context of the national accounts.

Before introducing the topic let us step back in history once more. Marginalism won over classical value theory for two reasons. One was mathematics, whose application to economics came by way of marginalist thought; the other was the unresolved distinction between use value and exchange value, exemplified by the coal–diamond paradox. It was noted in Chapter 1 that marginalism's claim to have resolved the paradox is not really valid since the prices of different commodities cannot be compared. Nevertheless the problem of the coexistence of different concepts of value is addressed in the reappraisal of classical value theory, made possible by mathematisation and input–output analysis. It is known there as the transformation problem.

Let an economy be given by its input coefficient table, $A = (a_{ij}, i = 1, \ldots n; j = 1, \ldots, n)$, where each a_{ij} indicates the amount of input of type i required for the production of a unit of type j. Almost every country is in possession of such a table, describing the division of labour in a market economy. But division of labour is not possible without capital. So there is another matrix, $B = (b_{ij}, i = 1, \ldots n; j = 1, \ldots, n)$, where each coefficient b_{ij} indicates the amount of capital of type i that is applied to the production of a unit of a good or service of type j. The ratio of the elements of the two matrices defines average turnover time, t_{ij} of capital i in use j:

$$\frac{b_{ij}}{a_{ij}} = t_{ij} \tag{8.32}$$

With these definitions one can define the following value system (Bródy, 1970):

$$l = v + lA \tag{8.33}$$

where v is the vector of labour income earned in each industry. The resulting vector, $l = (l_j, j = 1, \ldots n)$, can be called the labour value of product group j and interpreted as the employment needed in all branches combined to produce a unit of the final product (employment multipliers). But an input–output table of a modern economy also includes operating surplus, where the question arises of how to distribute it. Distributing the surplus in proportion to capital, the capital goods being themselves valued at corresponding prices, yields another value system, namely:

$$p = v + pA + \lambda pB \qquad (8.34)$$

These are called production prices, with λ as the uniform rate of profit in all industries (ibid.) Both price systems are artificial, of course. They are imputations made for the purpose of analysing the circuit of economic flows. Thus an accounting in labour values illustrates the flow of this production factor through the economy, because all values are counted in labour – 'resolved into labour' as the classicists say. Production prices, in contrast, show the circulation of capital through the economy, or more precisely the value of the means of production, 'dead labour' in classical terminology. In a simple competitive economy without a government sector these are the market prices, reflecting the phenomenon of value, or as Marx would say the 'surface' of value, of which the imputed labour values would represent the essence or content. Perhaps we could also interpret one of these value systems as the operationalisation of the classical 'value in use' and the other as 'value in exchange' to illustrate the distinction made by classical economists between different value concepts, but we shall leave this open. In any case it is clear that both models are fully proportionate, or as we say today, linear. Value does not depend on quantity, or as the national accountant says: a potato is a potato is a potato (in value), irrespective of the quantities produced. Instead value depends on the linkage between production processes, as represented by an input–output table. This dependence is not a simple matter, and is much more complex than the above equations may suggest. But this is not the point here. It is sufficient to show that the envisaged concept is based on the macro concept of economic circuit in place of microeconomic production functions.

Sraffa's model is equivalent to Equation 8.34, only Sraffa uses dated labour rather than turnover time for defining capital. The 'standard commodity' invented by Sraffa can be described as the dual vector to Equation 8.34, namely:

$$q = Aq + \lambda Bq + c \qquad (8.35)$$

where c is the final consumption vector of the economy and q is a vector of output, distinguished by the quality of reproducing itself in constant proportions (eigenvector); q is an artificial vector, too, and hard to determine empirically. It is therefore not surprising that Sraffa's standard commodity has not found its way from Cambridge to the City of London. But it answers Ricardo's quest for a mass of commodities as the general value standard. It is also, as Bródy (ibid.) shows, the proportion in which commodities must be produced in order to assure balanced growth of the economy, to which the system of production prices belong as the proper signals of allocation.

As this is not the place to deal with classical value theory in a systematic fashion, the above sketch will have to suffice. The interested reader is referred to the authors mentioned above. We want to show that in spite of the apparent artificiality of the classical price systems the underlying idea of a circuit of value, and hence of the possibility of 'dissolving' different forms of value into each other analytically, is embodied in the national accounts. Thus the duality of the legal institution and the physical establishment of production can be formally recognised in the two value systems of classical provenance distinguishing prices and values. Production prices reflect the first, namely the distribution of operating surplus in proportion to ownership. Labour values reflect the second in that they distribute value in proportion to the actual human activity demanded in production. And values lie behind prices, that is the essence of value is human activity (labor), while what appears at the actually observed surface of the economy as transactions is distributed in proportion to capital.

Labour values are not found in the national accounts. But there is an analogy pointing to a similar dualism of value. We first replace the interest rate, λ, on capital in Equation 8.34 by a rate of tax on production, perhaps in proportion to capital input or, more realistically, in proportion to output (sales tax). Equation 8.34 will have to be slightly modified, assuming consistent valuation throughout the system. If v in Equation 8.33 is defined as the net value added generated in each industry, this equation describes valuation 'at factor cost', as it was called in earlier versions of the SNA, and value is defined as the sum of the factor cost embodied in each product. Impose the product tax and you are in a system of type 8.34, where the surplus over factor cost is not distributed in proportion to the factors, so that the resulting product 'at market prices', as it was called earlier, differs from the product at factor cost. Early national accountants used to speak of the 'blowing up' of national product through indirect taxes, a notion that is explicable only in terms of a duality of values between production and marketing and is foreign to the unitary value system of microeconomics.

These visions of value go beyond what is usually presented in the national accounts and venture deep into input–output technique and analysis. But the general idea that prices can be linearly decomposed into different elements that added together yield the total is used throughout the national accounts, be it in the treatment of value added tax, the determination of trade and transport margins, or lately the indirect measurement of financial intermediary services (FISIM). The common idea shared by the national accounts and classical value theory is the dissolution of value into its factors, which is nothing but an application of the notion of economic circuit. Mathematically the notion is expressed by the decomposition of the Leontief inverse, $Q = (I - A)^{-1}$, needed for solving Equation 8.15:

$$l = vQ = v(I - A)^{-1} = v(I + A + A^2 + A^3 + \ldots)$$ (8.36)

This can be interpreted as determining the value, l, by the direct input of labour, v, into production, plus all the indirect inputs effected through the intermediate consumption of other products. It is akin to classical theory. In fact when Ricardo rejected the mass of commodities as a standard of value, he was looking for a particular commodity that would be produced with an average rate of profit instead. As the mathematical treatment by Sraffa shows, this is tantamount to taking a mass of commodities as standard, because together they contain an average profit, by definition. And so does the consumer price index actually chosen as the value standard of the national accounts, today.

9
Open Questions

As stated in the Introduction, the purpose of this book – of which the author and the reader have now reached the end – is twofold: to join economic concepts pursued in the legacy of Richard Stone with those inherited from Sraffa, and to be entertaining in this endeavour. In ancient Greece the enacting of a set of three tragedies was followed by one comedy. Although the reader may have been subjected to a tragic breakdown as a result being confronted with issues that are usually treated separately by the economics discipline, in this book the comedy does not follow. It will have to wait until a future date, as will some more serious questions that have sprung up in this book but not been answered.

First, if in the analysis of the measurement of value at the elementary observation level we have come to the conclusion (Chapter 5) that 'price' in the micreconomic sense is 'quality' in price statistics, while in price statistics 'price', often called 'the pure price component', refers to what in microeconomics is the numéraire, this produces a serious dilemma. It is not possible to sit back and just enjoy the discovery, leaving it to others to solve the contradiction. There are strong traditions in both fields and it is not easy to decide from which end a unifying bridge should be built and which materials should be employed.

Secondly, if the price and volume components of value, referring to specific product groups, depend on classification and aggregation, as we found in Chapter 4, how are these to be designed? Economic theory does not bother about such issues, leaving them to the statistical practitioner to decide. But if the growth rate of an economy depends on how its products are classified, some thought ought to be given to it.

Thirdly, our analysis has also shown that price and volume indices are concepts of disequilibrium rather than equilibrium, where these states refer to the relationship between markets and not to the conditions in each market, equilibrium in each market being incorporated into the measurement itself (Chapter 7). We have drawn the conclusion that price differences of this kind are usefully interpreted as a measure of scarcity. But scarcity is itself a dubious, ill-defined concept that needs to be put into a much clearer context in order to render this interpretation plausible.

Production, we argued in Chapter 3, is a human activity that is performed regularly and against pay. We may or may not have convinced the reader of this proposition. Mind you the point is not about what is the right definition, as the older productivity debates had it. It is not normative, it is descriptive in trying to analyse the conceptual essence of what in a primitive and untheoretical *ad hoc* manner one dubbs 'the SNA production boundary'. There must be more reason to it than a mere 'fiat'. But even if this concept is accepted, it must be shown how it can be implemented in practice, which has not been done in this book.

Finally, and most importantly, are there actually two theories of value, as suggested in Chapter 6, one for the microeconomic, the other for the macroeconomic realm? We hope to have made it fairly clear that the microeconomic theory dose not support the national accounts, and *vice versa*. But what can we do about it? Should each field proceed independently as a self-sufficient academic discipline? Can the fields be joined? Must they be joined? This is not a question of mathematics, of course. Formally the models of classical value theory can be joined with those of its neoclassical sucessors, these being couched in more general terms. But in terms of content, of the measurement operations standing behind the symbols entering into the formal structures, these questions must be asked.

The author is happy not to answer these questions, although they bothered him throughout the writing of the book. Expecting that the book will find its own fate after clearing the publisher, the author wishes it good luck. Writing it has been an entertaining exercise, and who knows where we will meet again.

Notes

1 Introduction: Why Write About Value in the Context of National Accounts?

1 Smith, A. (1776) p. 56.
2 Smith, A. (1776) p. 34.

2 Transactions and Their Economic Functions

1 They might be called liabilities to nature if the flow of values includes ecological concerns (see Chapter 8).
2 Every set of definitions must include some terms that are undefined. They are evident. Here the term 'event' is put in quotation marks to show this axiomatic quality, with a reference to Ludwig Wittgenstein's words in the tractatus logico-philisophicus: 'Die Welt ist alles, was der Fall ist' – the world is everything that happens.
3 This refers to pure credit transactions. Transactions in gold and securities are more complex and are therefore not discussed here.
4 In an illuminating paper, Kircher (1953) shows how closely the distinction between transactions to other units and value transformation within units is linked to business accounts.

3 Institutions and Their Economic Activities

1 The SNA also mentions the use of the locality criterion to provide 'a picture of the distribution of production in space' (para. 2.44). This refers to the possibility of constructing regional accounts. As this study is confined to the national level, we do not discuss that topic, apart from stating that for a complete system of accounts in the sense of the SNA, the national level (that is, the currency space) is indispensable. Regional, subnational and supranational accounts can only provide some of the aggregates defined in the system, and not the data for the complete economic circuit (Reich, 1996).
2 This refers to para. 6.6 of the 1993 SNA, which states that 'the economic analysis of production is mainly concerned with activities that produce outputs of a kind that can be delivered or provided to other institutional units'. The fact that goods transferred between the establishments of a single institututional unit are counted as part of output (and intermediate consumption), as stated later in para. 6.38, is an exception to the general rule, probably based on the indistinguishability between the users of such output in establishment-based production statistics.
3 The so-called GDP 'at market prices' still expresses this contradiction because it includes non-market production at cost. The usual rationale is that costs are close to market prices quantitatively speaking. But this argument is *ad hoc* and not theoretically founded, because conceptually, and in terms of value theory, costs are something quite different from prices.
4 Except, of course, if the telling of jokes is performed regularly and against pay.
5 This is more than a metaphor. If you stand on the bank of the River Cam and see how comparatively narrow it is you will wonder why such great economists as

Pierro Sraffa on its one side and Richard Stone on the other had so little influence on each other even though they were working on the same subject and using the same mathematical tools.

6 It may not be wise to call such activities 'own-account' because this implies the existence of a very formal device. An account is typically not kept by non-institutional actors.

7 More than just making trouble for a generation of national accountants, Pigou's continued use of the housewife example shows that he never did housework himself. If he had be would have discovered that doing it yourself or employing a stranger affect the nature of this work, even in respect of his study room.

8 The first sentence of the ILO extract presented in the SNA deserves critical attention: 'The informal sector may be broadly characterized as consisting of units engaged in the production of goods and services with the primary objective of generating employment and incomes to the persons concerned'. (para. 5.1). This definition is almost identical to that of its logical counterpart – the corporation (para. 4.23). The overlooked difference is that the units, as they are abstractly called, are not legal, property-owning and value-transacting institutions, but individual people or families with obviously different norms of behaviour. Consequently there is neither employment nor income in the sense of the system. Simply to call them that is at the least an unreflected hypothesis and at the most an ideological euphemism. Fortunately the subsequent statements clarify the point.

9 'Imputed values would not be equivalent to monetary values for analytic or policy purposes outside the market exchange' (SNA, 1993, para. 6.21).

4 The Index Number Problem

1 In the experience of the author, only 50 per cent of economics students, when asked to explain the meaning of the term 'real' in their final exam, give a correct answer in this sense.

2 For a more general analysis in terms of additivity see Cuthbert (1999).

3 Equations 4.2 and 4.3 correspond to Equations (1) and (4) in the UN *Handbook of the International Comparison Programme* (United Nations, 1992, p. 72 f). Purchasing power parity (PPP) is then given by PPP $= 1/\varepsilon$. We prefer to use ε because it can be interpreted as the real exchange rate as opposed to the nominal exchange rate, e.

4 For the true figures see United Nations and Commission of the European Communities (1994).

5 See for example Diewert (1993).

5 The Quality Problem

1 Actually, the assumption that the map of preferences is constant over time, although essential in traditional price theory, was criticised quite early in economic doctrine (Hicks, 1940, p.107 f). The theory of the superlative price index takes a useful step in that direction, by making the price index independent of utility functions up to the second order. It misses the next step, though, which would be to define price and value *a priori* to such unobservable functions.

2 See, for example, Diewert and Montmarquette (1982), Foreword.

3 Although the techniques are the same, their labels are different even among English-speaking countries. We choose the SNA terminology.

4 This expression is not very suitable, because in applying the splicing technique the prices of the two items are also directly compared but it is used in Statistics Canada (1995) and therefore here too.

5 This is a statement about common rules. Lack of data often results in choosing a different order of calculations, but this is a matter of practicality and approximative techniques rather than principle.

Bibliography

Archambault, E. (1994) *Comptabilité nationale*, 5th edn (Paris: Economica).

Abraham-Frois, G. and E. Berelli (1976) *Theory of Value, Prices and Accumulation. A Mathematical Integration of Marx, von Neumann and Sraffa* (Cambridge: Cambridge UP).

Becker, G. S. (1964) *Human Capital: A Theoretical and Empirical Analysis With Special Reference To Education* (New York: McGraw-Hill).

Becker, G. S. (1981) *A Treatise On The Family* (Cambridge, London: Harvard UP).

Bochove, C. A. van and H. K. van Tuinen (1986) 'Flexibility in the Next SNA: The Case for an Institutional Core', *The Review of Income and Wealth*, vol. 32 (June), pp. 127–54.

Boskin, M. J., E. R. Dulberger, R. J. Gordon, Z. Griliches and D. Jorgensen (1998) 'Toward a More Accurate Measure in the Cost of Living', in D. Baker (ed.), *Getting Prices Right. The Debate Over the Consumer Price Index* (New York and London: M. E. Sharpe), pp. 5–77.

Bródy, A. (1970) *Proportions, Prices and Planning* (Amsterdam: North-Holland).

Brümmerhoff, D. (1995) *Volkswirtschaftliche Gesamtrechnung*, 5th edn (Munich and Vienna: R. Oldenbourg Verlag).

Calzaroni, M., E. Giovanni and V. Madelin (1996) 'Exhaustiveness of GDP Measurement: French and Italian Approaches', paper presented to the 24th General Conference of the International Association for Research in Income and Wealth, Lillehammer, Norway, 18–24 August.

Chapron, J.-E. and M. Séruzier (1984) *Initiation pratique à la comptabilité nationale selon le nouveau système* (Paris: Masson).

Choudhury, U. D. R. (1986) 'Comments on the Overall Programme', *The Review of Income and Wealth*, vol. 32 (June), pp. 122–26.

Cuthbert, J. R. (1999) 'Categorisation of additive purchasing power parities', *The Review of Income and Wealth*, vol. 45 June, pp. 235–49.

Debreu, G. (1959) *Theory of Value. An Axiomatic Analysis of Economic Equilibrium* (New Haven and London: Yale University Press).

Diewert, W. E. (1993) 'The Early History of Price Index Research', in W. E. Diewert and A. O. Nakamura (eds) *Essays in Index Numbers* vol. 1 (Amsterdam: North-Holland), pp. 33–65.

Diewert, W. E. and C. Montmarquette (eds) (1982) *Price level measurement: proceedings from a conference sponsored by Statistics Canada* (Ottawa: Statistics Canada).

Eck, R. von, C. N. Gorter and H. K. van Tuinen (1983) *Flexibility in the system of national accounts*, National Accounts Occasional Paper no. NA-01 (Voorburg: Netherlands Central Bureau of Statistics).

Eichhorn, W. and J. Voeller (1976) *Theory of the Price Index* (Berlin, Heidelberg, New York: Springer).

Eichhorn, W. *et al.* (eds) (1978) *Theory and Applications of Economic Indices* (Würzburg: Physica).

Eisner, R. (1995) 'Expansion of Boundaries and Satellite Accounts', in J. W. Kendrick (ed.), *The New System of National Accounts* (Boston, Dordrecht and London: Kluwer Academic Publishers), pp. 91–113.

ESA (1995), Commission of the European Union, *European System of National Accounts*, Brussels.

Fisher, I. (1927) *The Making of Index Numbers* (Boston: Houghton Mifflin).

Frank, R. H. (1991) *Microeconomics and Behavior* (New York: McGraw-Hill).

Frenkel, M., and K. D. John (1991) *Volkswirtschaftliche Gesamtrechnung* (Munich: Verlag Franz Vahlen).

Gablers Wirtschaftslexikon (1988) 12th edn (Wiesbaden: Gabler Verlag).

Goldschmidt-Clermont, L. and E. Pagnossin-Aligisakis (1996) 'Measuring Non-SNA Economic Activities: Potential and Limitations of Time Use Data', paper presented to the 24th General Conference of the International Association for Research in Income and Wealth, Lillehammer, Norway, 18–24 August.

Gorter, C. N. (1988) *Imputations and re-routings in the national accounts*, National Accounts Occasional Paper no. NA-026 (Voorburg: Netherlands Central Bureau of Statistics).

Hawrylyshyn, O. (1977) 'Towards a Definition of Non-Market Activities', *The Review of Income and Wealth*, vol. 23, pp. 79–96.

Hicks, J. (1940) *Value and Capital* (Oxford: Oxford UP)

Hill, T. P. (1977) 'On goods and services', *The Review of Income and Wealth*, vol. 23, pp. 315–38.

Holub, H.-W. (1994) 'Produktion', in D. Brümmerhoff and H. Lützel (eds), *Lexikon der Volkswirtschaftlichen Gesamtrechnungen* (Munich and Vienna: R. Oldenbourg Verlag), pp. 283–5.

Horvat, B. (1995) *The Theory of Value, Capital and Interest. A New Approach* (Aldershot: Edward Elgar).

Hulten, C. R. (1995) 'Capital and Wealth in the Revised SNA', in J. W. Kendrick (ed.), *The New System of National Accounts* (Boston, Mass.: Kluwer), pp. 149–81.

INSEE (1996) Institut National de la Statistique et des Etudes Economiques, *Instruction détaillée aux enquêteurs des prix à la consommation des ménages* (Paris: INSEE).

Jevons, W. S. (1911) *The Theory of Political Economy* (London: Macmillan).

Kendrick, J. W. (1995) 'Introduction and Overview', in J. W. Kendrick (ed.), *The New System of National Accounts* (Boston, Mass.: Kluwer), pp. 1–23.

Keynes, J. M. (1936) *The General Theory of Employment, Interest and Money* (London, New York: Harcourt, Brace & World).

Kircher, P. (1953) 'Accounting entries and national accounts', *The Accounting Review*, vol. xxviii, pp. 191–8.

Kravis, I. B., A. Heston and R. Summers (1983) *World Product and Income. International Comparisons of Real Gross Product* (Baltimore, MD: Johns Hopkins University Press).

Lancaster, K. (1973) *Modern Economics: Principles and Policy* (Chicago, Ill.: Rand McNally).

Lipsey, G. L. and P. O. Steiner (1981) *Economics*, 6th edn (New York: Harper & Row).

Lowry, S. T. (1974) 'The archeology of the circulation concept in economic theory', *Journal of the History of Ideas*, vol. xxxv, pp. 429–44.

Marhoum, R. (1996) 'Evaluation critique du champ de la production du sytème des comptes économiques algériens et nécessités d'adaption au sytème des comptes normalisés O.N.U 1993', *Bulletin de l'association de comptabilité nationale*, no. 30 (Paris: INSEE, 9 May), pp. 2–10.

McConnell, C. R. (1984) *Economics: Principles, Problems, and Policies* (New York: McGraw-Hill).

Mulder, N. (1996) 'Accounting for Informality: the Case of Brazil and Mexico', paper presented to the 24th General Conference of the International Association for Research in Income and Wealth, Lillehammer, Norway, 18–24 August.

Müller, F. (1984) *Volkswirtschaftliche Gesamtrechnungen und Preisveränderungen. Untersuchungen auf der Basis einer Neufassung des Aggregatsbegriffs, mit einem preisbereinigten Kontensystem für die Bundesrepublik Deutschland* (Hain, Hanstein and Königstein/Ts: Athenäum).

Oladoye, J. O. (1996) 'Production Boundary in the Informal Sector: The Experience of Nigeria', paper presented to the 24th General Conference of the International Association for Research in Income and Wealth, Lillehammer, Norway, 18–24 August.

Rashidi, Abibu (1996) 'Analyse et évaluation du secteur informel au Zaire', *Bulletin de l'association de comptabilité nationale*, no. 30, 18–22 (Paris: 9 INSEE, May), pp. 18–22.

Reich, U.-P. (1989) 'Essence and Appearance: Reflections on Input–Ouput Methodology in Terms of a Classical Paradigm', *Economic Systems Research*, vol. 1 no. 4, pp. 417–28.

Reich, U.-P. (1996) 'Der Raumbegriff der Volkswirtschaftlichen Gesamtrechnungen: Folgerungen aus dem Transaktionsprinzip', in U.-P. Reich, C. Stahmer and K. Voy (eds), *Kategorien der Volkswirtschaftlichen Gesamtrechnungen, Band 1, Raum und Grenzen* (Marburg: Metropolis Verlag), pp. 73–110.

Ricardo, D. (1951) 'Absolute Value and Exchangeable Value', in P. Sraffa (ed.), *The Works and Correspondence of David Ricardo*, vol. IV, pamphlets and papers (Cambridge: Cambridge UP).

Rieter, H. (1990) 'Quesnays Tableau Economique als Uhrenanalogie', *Schriften des Vereins für Socialpolitik*, vol. 115, pp. 57–94.

Ruggles, N. D. and R. Ruggles (1982) 'Integrated Economic Accounts for the United States, 1947–80', *Survey of Current Business*, vol. 62, no. 5, pp. 1–53.

Ruggles, R. (1961) 'Measuring the cost of quality. How realistic is the consumer price index', *Challenge. The Magazine of Economic Affairs* vol. X, no. 2.

Ruggles, R. (1995) 'The United Nations System of National Accounts and the Integration of Macro and Micro Data', in J. W. Kendrick (ed.), *The New System of National Accounts* (Boston, Mass.: Kluwer), pp. 387–416.

Sachs, D. J. and F. B. Larrain (1993) *Macroeconomics in the Global Economy* (Englewood Cliffs, NJ: Prentice Hall).

Salvatore, D. (1994) *Microeconomics*, 2nd edn (New York: HarperCollins).

Samuelson, P. A. and W. D. Nordhaus (1989) *Economics*, 13th edn (New York: McGraw-Hill).

Smith, A. (1776), *An Inquiry into the Nature and Causes of the Wealth of Nations* (London)

SNA (1993) Commission of the European Communities, International Monetary Fund, Organisation for Economic Co-operation and Development, United Nations and World Bank, *System of National Accounts 1993* (Brussels, New York, Paris and Washington, DC).

Sraffa, P. (1960) *Production of Commodities by Means of Commodities* (Cambridge: Cambridge UP).

Statistics Canada (1995) *The Consumer Price Index Reference Paper. Update Based On 1992 Expenditures* (Ottawa: Statistics Canada).

Stobbe, A. (1994) *Volkswirtschaftliches Rechnungswesen*, 8th edn (Berlin: Springer Verlag).

Stone, J. R. N. and J. E. Meade (1944) *National Income and Expenditure* (London, Cambridge: Cambridge UP).

Stone, R. (1951) 'Functions and Criteria of a System of Social Accounting', in. E. Lundberg (ed.), *Income and Wealth*, series I (Cambridge: Bowes and Bowes), pp. 1–74.

Studenski, P. (1958) *The Income of Nations. Part One: History, Part Two: Theory and Methodology*, 2nd edn (New York: Macmillan).

Teichert, V. (1993) *Das informelle Wirtschaftssystem. Analyse und Perspektiven von Erwerbs- und Eigenarbeit* (Opladen: Westdeutscher Verlag).

Todaro, M. P. (1989) *Economic Development in the Third World* (New York: Longman).

United Nations (1992) *Handbook of the International Comparison Programme*, series F, no. 62 (New York: UN).

United Nations and Commission of the European Communities (1994) *World Comparisons of Real Gross Domestic Product and Purchasing Power, 1985*, phase v of the International Comparison Programme (New York).

Vries, W. F. M. de, G. P. den Bakker, M. B. G. Gircour, S. J. Keuning and A. Lenson (eds) (1993) *The Value Added of National Accounting. Commemorating 50 years of national accounts in the Netherlands* (Voorburg/Heerlen: Netherlands Central Bureau of Statistics).

Walras, L. (1874) *Eléments d'économie politique pure ou théorie de la richesse sociale* (Paris: Pichon & Durand-Auzias).

Index